CHRIST
AND THE CHRISTIAN

CHRIST
AND THE CHRISTIAN

BY

NELS F. S. FERRÉ

Abbot Professor of Christian Theology
Andover Newton Theological School

HARPER & BROTHERS · NEW YORK

Library of Congress catalog card number: 58-5192

To

John Keith and Lois Benton
friends and co-workers

CONTENTS

Preface

CONTENTS

PREFACE

THERE are two keys to *Christ and the Christian*. The first is the relation between encounter and co-inherence. God is not a spiritual Personality but a personal Spirit. Only when this contrast is fully explained can the truth become convincing that God was both truly beyond and truly in Jesus. In a genuine sense, then, Jesus is understood as both Son of Man and Son of God. The second key to the book is that the historic Incarnation involves all mankind, whose proper, potential relation to God is incarnation. This volume is therefore correctly named *Christ and the Christian*.

Interestingly, quite opposite criticisms are frequently made of this analysis: it is too special; it is too general. Keen critics claim that what I present as a decisive, historic event in Jesus can, in fact, be found in non-Christian religions. Let such critics produce the evidence. For years I have sought for such facts, for I have a historian's dread of "making a case" for Christianity. Truth alone will stand. My attempt is to take history with all seriousness, although recognizing that historicity is a most difficult subject to treat. The critics who assail me for being too general, on the other hand, want me to produce a unique Christ and a unique Christian faith. I am a Christian, however, only because I am convinced that God is Agape. When I come to Him as the ultimate Reality and Truth, I cannot but see all things in the Light of Who He is. As a matter of fact, I am increasingly impressed by the fact that encounter as a personal category and co-inherence as a spiritual category underlie man's total relation to God. Christology, for me, is consequently both special and general truth. The general, however, is far easier to establish than the special, and on both points I am open to suggestions for improvement.

Even while a candidate for the doctorate I was intensely interested in Christology, both as a matter of personal decision and as a matter of general truth. One of the earliest books I thought of writing bore the imaginary title: Metaphysical Implications of Early Christology. I used to ponder with amazement, even as a student of philosophy, the deep and wide general truths that were indicated by the theological positions of the Early Church Fathers. In preparation for the present volume I naturally returned to the Fathers for rereading and further reading. Once again I was convicted of their depth of insight in comparison to most of our modern dealing with Christology. The general truth of incarnation weighed heavily and worthily in their thinking. The two modern works that have helped me the most are Prestige's *Fathers and Heretics* and Singh's *Preface to Personality*. Both books are strong in their emphasis on the historic and the general truths of Christology. To the already well-thumbed *Ante-Nicene Fathers* and the *Nicene and Post-*

Nicene Fathers, I added the choice material in the *Library of Christian Classics.*

Christ and the Christian was originally prepared as the Centennial Lectures at Louisville Presbyterian Seminary in 1955. Can a theologian be more honored than to have the centennial class of a seminary invite him to give the commemorative lectures? During my stay there the faculty informally elected me an "honorary member" and introduced me as such. The graciousness of this gesture warmed me through and through. At the end of the fourth lecture, "Christ and the Christian," Professor Rule told me he had heard I was heretical, but that up to this point I was as orthodox as he! Since I had heard that he was the most "conservative" professor at the seminary my feelings at his observation were at first mixed until I realized that the very truth of classical Christology at its center unites both the conservative and the progressive. His informal, obviously generous remarks made me deeply grateful and hopeful, as well, that this volume will help to bring together all honest and informed seekers who struggle with the depth of historic truth and with the needs for intellectual integrity and adequacy on the part of modern man. *Christ and the Christian* is written in this spirit and for this purpose.

When I was asked to give the Earl Lectures a second time at the Pacific School of Religion, I was deeply moved. These lectures were postponed for a year to take advantage of Emil Brunner's presence in America. Meanwhile the natural subject of my choice became the Christology on which I had by then started to work. To give the Earl Lectures is a great experience if only because of the hundreds of ministers who come from the Western States and Canada. I was thankful for my warm reception in Berkeley in 1956, but I was a bit taken aback by a rather strong objection to the lecture on the Atonement. The comment was generally that on this topic I was trying to please the Fundamentalists. Let the record of my writings speak for itself on that point! When I returned home I searched both mind and heart in the light of this criticism, but the original treatment had to stand. The Atonement, to be correctly interpreted, should be considered as both conclusive and inclusive. Ways of interpreting the facts may change but I am genuinely convinced that God has done something for us and will keep doing something for us that we cannot do for ourselves. For me the Atonement stands for the fact that we live by faith and grace, not by intellectual wisdom or moral endeavor; and that God's acceptance is first of all due to His own accepting us and providing the conditions for such acceptance. Similarly, I cannot reach any conclusion but that Resurrection is real. Not only did God raise Jesus from the dead but we await our own resurrection. But Resurrection whether special or general depends on a kind of life, on a kind of relation to God that should begin in this life.

A third set of Foundation lectures on Christology was presented at the Western Theological Seminary in Pittsburgh as the Elliott Lectures in 1957. Thus my Christology was written and given mostly under Presbyterian auspices. The

Presbyterians have a high view of theology that makes it a privilege to work with them. Their God-centeredness is also most hospitable to my witness. All from president to students received me with warmth and seriousness while maintaining a critical openness to my message. Pittsburgh for me now means much depth of theological seriousness.

I have spoken on Christology over the last few years in too many places to mention. A few, however, should be acknowledged. My students at Vanderbilt have witnessed almost every new discovery as it has been given me. In the same way the students at the Hartley Victoria Methodist College in Manchester, England, where I was privileged to be an exchange teacher, patiently encouraged my wrestling with Christological themes. Some of the material was likewise given at Edinburgh, Scotland, in sermons and in a lecture at New College under the sponsorship of the Scottish Congregational College, and at Trinity College of the University of Glasgow, before the Glasgow Theological Society. In Canada, the places where I have particularly dealt with the subject are Union College at the University of British Columbia, Union College in Winnipeg, and the National Conference on Evangelism at Whitby, Ontario. In the United States the subject has been treated in innumerable places, but especially, in part, at Princeton Theological Seminary; at Methodist Pastors' Schools from coast to coast; twice at Roanoke, Virginia, once under burning circumstances; at Bridgewater College, Church of the Brethren, Virginia; and at the Pastors' School of the Michigan Council of Churches.

The long chapter on "The Humanity of Jesus" was written as an assignment for the Committee on Christ and His Church, of the Faith and Order Commission of the World Council of Churches. It was carefully discussed at the Seabury House meeting of the Committee in the summer of 1955. The four people who offered especially helpful criticisms were Paul Minear, Robert Calhoun, Norman Pittinger, and Claude Welch. The following summer the paper was studied by the European Section of the Committee, in its meeting at Oxford, England. There critical discussion proved also of immense help to me, especially that of Thomas Torrance of Edinburgh, Edmund Schlink of Heidelberg and Gustaf Wingren of Lund. Some of the discussion is included in the book.

The two who have helped me the most intimately, however, are my former colleagues, Langdon Gilkey and Roger Shinn. After reading their written criticisms, chapter by chapter, I have become ever more thankful for their advice. Both of them urged me to rewrite the third section of the first chapter since this is crucial to my whole position. I am especially grateful for their frankness and thoroughness.

Thus I have been helped by many. Nevertheless it must be obvious that no one is to be thought of as agreeing with my position in any part or as a whole. The final weight of responsibility must rest on me. I must admit, however, that recently I have been pleased beyond expression by a new understanding and acceptance in many areas that I had not expected. In extreme circles irresponsible and often uninformed, accusations are still being hurled, but I believe that even there by now constructive intelligence is getting the upper hand over unthinking fanaticism. My main intention in writing this volume is to show how relevant and real is classical Christianity when it is taken at its own heart.

This time my wife has worked with me more closely than ever. We have read aloud every word of the book in an attempt to make it as easy reading as possible without forfeit of theological seriousness. Mrs. Harold Kieler has once more typed draft after draft with unwearied patience. I should like to express thanks to them both. I have, however, checked all the notes myself and if there are any errors I am alone responsible for them! Once again I acknowledge my continued indebtedness to all the members of Harper's Religious Books Department, whose sound advice and unflagging interest set ever higher standards of achievement.

In dedicating this book to the late Dean Benton and Mrs. Benton, I am expressing a debt I can never pay. His faith in me made possible a program of research and writing that was most unusual, if rivaled anywhere in the world. In leaving Vanderbilt we leave behind us a large number of irreplaceable friends. Southern friendliness lasts; I now have proof of that. I owe a debt of gratitude, too, to all my colleagues, for they have been a real source of help and comfort to me. My return to Andover Newton Theological School as Abbot Professor touches me at my deepest springs of affection. Particularly I can never forget how the late

President Herrick and Dean Dabney stood by me through periods of illness that seemed dark indeed, and how Dean Pearson, as a student in my first class, chauffeured and all but carried me to classes daily for a year, for no reward save friendship and a common witness.

As to future writing I make no specific promises or predictions. My longing is from now on to deal with two fields: the general questions of the meaning of existence and the reality of faith for modern man, and the relations of the Christian faith to the religions of the world. All that, however, is in God's hands. More and more I am impressed with the reality and power of faith and with the endless grace of God, while less and less I feel worthy and adequate to deal with Him and His truth. Whatever in my theological writing may be helpful I owe entirely to His unmerited grace.

NELS F. S. FERRÉ

Newton, Massachusetts
July 2, 1957

CHRIST
AND THE CHRISTIAN

I

WHERE DO WE START?

THE theological curriculum converges on the subject of
Christ. Bible, Church history, theology and even the "practical" subjects center in him. The theological school and the
church are bound together by their allegiance to him. The
preacher in the pulpit and the layman in the pew carry on
their Christian vocations in his name and for his sake. He
is not only the focal point of the Church's faith but also
the living heart of every believer's confession. The outside
world, too, that may ignore the seminary and despise the
church, cannot readily forget or avoid "the strange man on
the Cross" who changed the calendar of our Western world.
The humblest worshiper, the most exalted teacher of the
Christian faith, and even the rejector of the Christian claim
confront the fact of the Christ, for his nonexpungeable
presence in our history and in our deepest selves bids us
decide concerning him.

It is important, therefore, to be extremely careful in

19

choosing the method of approach to a subject. The method we use may make or may break our theology, for the method may itself determine the result. A wrong method works the more harm the more conscientiously and competently it is used. Surely Robert Barclay is right when he writes: "In this affair then should our inquiry be the more diligent, because he that errs in the entrance is not so easily brought back again into the right way; he that misseth his road from the beginning of his journey, and is deceived in his first marks, at his first setting forth, the greater his mistake is, the more difficult will be his entrance into the right way." [1]

The great and good Edgar Brightman, for instance, mostly on account of method concluded that God was finite. He believed truth to be governed by the whole of knowledge. If God is understood as completely good, Brightman inferred, and stated forthrightly, then the dark evils of this world prove that He is not also all-powerful. Indeed, only a different method can allow an honest and competent mind to arrive at the sovereign God as saving Love.

Similarly, Kierkegaard's original methodological assumption has caused a radical disintegration of the historical Jesus in much of the New Testament studies of this century. Kierkegaard made the "infinite qualitative distinction" between eternity and time a main presupposition of his thinking. Therefore he concluded that "from history one can learn nothing about Christ" [2] and that "knowledge demolishes

[1] *An Apology for the Christian Divinity*, p. 23.
[2] *Training in Christianity*, p. 28.

Jesus Christ." [3] Karl Barth, in turn, made this same presupposition central to his epoch-making *Epistle to the
Romans*. New Testament scholars thereupon became deeply
imbued with this assumption and soon reflected this thesis
in their writings. Rudolf Bultmann, for instance, strikingly
illustrates the power of Kierkegaard's original methodological assumption.

Or again, Paul Tillich grew tired of waking up morning
after morning wondering what historical scholarship in the
New Testament field had done to his theology. He therefore
lifted his own Christology to such a high point of construction that he could claim that it makes no difference whether
or not Jesus could be known, for Christ is still the perfect
synthesis of essence and existence. The picture of the Christ
reveals for us an existence transparent to essence. In him
meaning and history coincide. Tillich believes that his own
method of correlation, wherein philosophy asks the questions
and theology answers them, bears out demonstrably his
claim for Christ as the center of history.

Some time ago, moreover, Henry Joel Cadbury laid bare
"the peril of modernizing Jesus." He showed with much
truth that each generation tends to think of Jesus in terms
of its own ideals rather than to subject its own fondest
thinking to the brute facts of first-century Palestine. Some,
however, upon reading his book, felt equally the peril of
reducing Jesus to a typical member of his own first-century

[3] *Ibid.*, p. 36.

environment;[4] and felt also that Dr. Cadbury's historical picture of Jesus reflected not a little the attitude of a contemporary member of the Society of Friends!

These illustrations suffice to give us pause at the beginning of our task. All the men that we have mentioned are strong, mature thinkers. Is it possible, then, to get beyond our personal slants and our social background? Certainly we cannot hope to do so entirely, but we can at least take every precaution, and, being aware of the danger, attempt to avoid it as far as possible. We can learn humility and the "folly of discharging intellectualist wisecracks at opponents who are talking a different theological language."[5]

We can also learn that Christology is the serious study of life at its center. It concerns the questions not only of ultimate reality and meaning but also of everyday life with its duties and satisfactions. Calvin knew full well that Christology was no study of alchemy or chemistry in the abstract. It is never merely a matter of this and that part of Christ making a new Being. Christology, rather, has this subjective side: the cry of the human heart in its deepest need for God. It is the working of the mind at its highest pitch with regard to its basic task, the problem of life and death, the meaning of existence and the center of all our decisions. Christology aloof from life's actual problems and powers:

[4] If we have to reduce a man's meaning to customary use of terms, no creative advance would ever be possible apart from a totally new language. Therefore Jesus may not be reduced to a typical member of his time because of his use of ordinary terms. Words get new meanings from context and illustrations.

[5] G. L. Prestige, *Fathers on Heretics*, p. 128.

our individual troubles, heartaches and hopes; our social struggles of race, nations, social groupings, religions, denominations, and vested interests—such a Christology is dry bones both for thought and faith. But in the end we know that the subjective demands and promises are not enough unless what is actually there, the objective side of Christology, comes both as a deadly threat to every form of evil and also as healing light and power to every honest and open spirit, and to every people looking for the coming of the Kingdom of God.

The study of Christ is also basically important because many of our archetypal assumptions of thought and culture are wrapped up inside the bundle of this historic faith. Civilization moves largely upon unconscious assumptions. Many believers and unbelievers have no idea what is involved in their faith with regard both to depth-response of life and to cultural coloration. For nearly two thousand years Christian assumptions have shaped much of Western thinking; while, on the other hand, alien problems of life and civilization have found a subconscious covert behind many so-called "Christian" formulations. The corruption of the best is the worst form of social and cultural frustration. Therefore there is need to face the Christological formulations themselves to find what is real and true, and to fortify with such discovery our personal and cultural lives. There is further need to detect what is warped and untrue in order to rid civilization of its false assumptions that are protected behind heretical Christologies. What may seem "stuffy theology" or technical quibbling may in fact represent archetypal forms of subconscious response. This fact should constantly be kept in mind upon the reading of this volume.

The least we can do to start with, in any case, is to examine several possible starting points or methods of approach and to indicate why these will not do; and why we start where we do, namely, with Christ himself as Agape,[6] the Event-Meaning that can most fully explain existence, most searchingly tells us what is wrong with it, and, above all, most fully indicate how all things can be made right. First, however, we shall consider where we should not start methodologically and for what reasons.

I. SHOULD WE START WITH OUR EXPERIENCE OF CHRIST?

In one sense the above question answers itself. How can we possibly escape starting with our own experience and how can we ever get beyond it? The real import of the question, however, is different. It is rather this: Can we afford to let our own experience of Christ become determinative for Christology? If we start with our experience as the basic fact, we certainly shall have a hard time, in any case, ever getting beyond it. How is it possible to get beyond our own experience as the starting point of our investigation? Even though we have to start with experience *psychologically,* is our experience of Christ the right place to begin for our theological method? *Methodologically* should we, or must

[6] Agape, of course, is the New Testament Greek word for the distinctive love that came with Christ.

we, start with our experience of Christ or can we go beyond it to a more adequate point of beginning?

What of individual experience as the starting point? Did not St. Paul build his knowledge of Christ on the fact that he had himself been confronted with the living Christ? Did he not assert that he did not go up to Jerusalem to seek out the other apostles nor did he seek his revelation from flesh and blood, but rather he went out into Arabia where alone with Christ he could develop his understanding of the Faith? When William Adams Brown, a leading American theologian of the past generation, had finished a whole week's lectures on Christ, he was startled to be asked: "But what does Jesus mean to you personally?" The questioner wanted the ring of personal experience of Christ and not merely theories concerning him. Peter Taylor Forsyth, too, confessed that Christ never became alive for him until he "was turned from a Christian to a believer, from a lover of love to an object of grace." [7]

In appraisal of individual experience as the starting point for the study of Christ, we must go beyond our admission that we cannot help starting here, since we can never escape from the present fact of our own selves. We have to affirm also that our kind of experience may be a condition partly determining whether or not we can truly study Christ. Ignorance, it is true, may prevent genuine study, but far more important is the fact that sin may block real seeing. The rebellious and insecure person so dreads the judgment

[7] *Positive Preaching and the Modern Mind*, p. 193.

of the white light of God that in his depth-response he tries to see white as black. He therefore misrepresents the facts to himself, picks out some that support his interpretation to the exclusion of those that do not, and then twists together some picture of the Christ which will enable him both to evade the true Christ and to agree generally with many good things that are said about Him. Reason is never blank. It depends on experience. And experience is generally organized by the self in the interest of the self. Therefore the sinful self cleverly distorts the picture of Christ. For this reason, although we must pay precautionary heed to experience, even to individual experience, nevertheless, we should not make the experience itself, as interpreted by the self, the methodological starting point for a theological study of Christ.

What we have just considered is the sinner's experience. Obviously this can block a forthright study of Christ. As a matter of fact true experience of Christ is lacking! But what of the experience of Christ of the saint, as defined by the New Testament—one who is no longer under the dominion of sin? In the first place we theologians may not be saints even in this New Testament sense! At least we frequently seem more aware of the problem of Christ than of his power. Secondly, when the faith of the New Testament is victorious in us, we know that it is not our *experience* of Christ that matters but our experience of *Christ*. Then, again, even victorious experience as inward or intuitive knowledge is hard to translate into an objective method. Of course the theological writer can go beyond testimony—such as St. Paul's or Forsyth's—and use some agelong device for escaping the predicament of an egocentric beginning, such as idealism or existentialism.

The difficulty with idealism—which stresses that only like can know like and that therefore only mind can know mind, starting thus with mind or with self—is that usually the method starting with the mind's experience predetermines the result, for the self stays within itself by stressing itself as the criterion of truth. Such is not its intention, to be sure; it intends, rather, to get to the objective world by means of analogy and inference, or by intuitive identification. The psychological weight of certainty, however, seems to center so heavily in the self from the start, that it can never become free of itself in order to become governed by objective reality. In the case of a Christian idealism, wherein the beginning is made with our experience of Christ and the step is then taken to the objective Christ, the more *our experience* is stressed, the more the method bogs down in the psychocentricity of idealism; whereas the more the emphasis is put on our experience of *Christ,* the more natural it is to start with him anyway.

Existentialism, too, makes decision rather than reasoning central to knowledge. The self stands responsibly alone and must choose what is truth in order to know it. Again, however, the self that purports to leap free into reality is practically always the nervous leaper that falls right back into its own selfhood. The Christ who comes to us is far more reliable and real than the Christ to whom we leap! Existentialism is supposed to be a method, but subtly it becomes a metaphysics. Thus both idealism and existentialism land us in subjectivism. To start with the self is usually never to escape from the self; to begin with experience is practically always to be limited by experience.

An individualistic approach to experience, however, is not the only one. Can we perhaps begin with the experience of the people of God? Is not the faith of the Church the right place to set out? The Swedish theologians of the Lund School, often called "Lundensians," men like Aulén, Nygren, and Wingren, do just this. They begin with "the faith," *tron,* and claim to have no theological task that is not the exposition of "the faith" from its Agape center.

A practical negative illustration of such a use of an objective "Church-faith" is an account given by a clergyman present at a ministerial meeting in Stockholm. When a speaker asserted vehemently that we must preach the actual Resurrection and actual life after death as the hope of man and of the world, the minister who gave the report of this meeting leaned forward and questioned the speaker: "I did not think that you believed in life after death, from what you have told me personally. Why then are you so insistent on this message from the pulpit?" "Oh," came the reply, "I do not preach my personal faith, but the faith of the Church!" This illustration may suggest a possible fringe use of the faith of the Church. Is not the collective experience of the Church, however, a corrective of personal experience; and should we perhaps start with such collective experience of Christ on the part of the Church?

Outstanding theologians, like Barth in his *Doctrine of the Word of God,* begin with the exposition of the faith of the Church. Biblical theology becomes Church theology. Barth writes *Kirkliche Dogmatik,* Church doctrine. America's outstanding theologian, Reinhold Niebuhr, similarly aims to bear witness to the biblical faith of the Church at its inner core and reality. The biblical standard may not now be taken apart from the broad and deep experience of the Church.[8] One of America's leading New Testament scholars, John Knox, among others, has spent many years proving that if we are to understand Jesus we must not isolate the revelatory event of Jesus' life from that of the community of those who received and interpreted him. We know Jesus as those involved in the Christian community of faith and lose the fullness of Christ when we fail to acknowledge and to use this basic fact. None of these theologians, however, except the Lundensians, relies wholly on the descriptive approach whereby the Church's interpretation of the faith becomes determinative for method. Their methods are rather *configurative* and demand also the subjective response of faith. All that this means, however, is that collective and personal

[8] Edward Carnell in writing his doctoral dissertation at Harvard on Niebuhr's theology (*The Concepts of Dialectic in the Theology of Reinhold Niebuhr*) concluded that this stress on the total stream of the experience of the Church was enormously important in Niebuhr's basic approach. Obviously Niebuhr stresses "biblical theology" not individualistically but rather within this larger framework of the ongoing faith of the Church.

experience are combined. To be sure, in some cases the word "experience" is deeply disliked and emphasis is placed on the Holy Spirit. In fact, however, if biblical theology is Church theology, collective experience is of critical importance methodologically.

In proposing collective experience as a necessary starting-point, how can we help being involved in the thought forms and feeling-powers of our own age? Our thoughts are both suggested to us and limited by the kinds of interests and problems that belong to our times. No man, however universal in intention and interests, escapes being related to his world, and every man must therefore always in some real measure be interpreted by it. Obviously too, without commitment and involvement on the part of a community no thinker is ever understood enough to be accepted and to have his thoughts perpetuated. No historic figure, furthermore, can be seen except against the light of his interpreters. Who knows the truth about Mary Todd Lincoln? How very much of that famous figure depends now for its understanding or its misunderstanding upon the reports of a probably prejudiced reporter. Can a controversial figure like Christ, therefore, be known apart from the strong bias of those who reported his life? Such is the case with history. Is it not even more true not only that the Christian community today is committed to the Christ, but that some of its members are pathologically defensive of its Christ-figure? Granted that there can be no presuppositionless thinking and that without commitment to Christ there must be rebellion against him, nevertheless to start with collective experience in the study of Christ is to evade the whole question of objective fact.

In some sense, then, we must begin the study of Christology with experience, even with collective experience, and yet at the same time we cannot really begin there, in any basic sense. Collective experience must itself be subjected to a more adequate starting point for the theological investigation of the reality and meaning of Christ. Collective experience is too much subject to the charge of artificially constructing doctrine, whether by creative imagination fired by devotion, or by defensive rationalization, to be accepted as reliable.[9] Those who know the history of Mariology, for instance, known how the weighty theologians stood shoulder to shoulder against its uncontrolled growth, but how the pious monks and the simple devotion of the people kept pushing along the glorification uncontrollably until today we have, even officially, the doctrine of the Bodily Assumption. There seems to be need for such myths and symbols which are fashioned in the depths of the collective subconscious and erupt with uncontrollable appeal. Unconscious assumptions that become formulated as dogmas eventuate in dogmatic attitudes that crush ruthlessly the puny efforts of factual or moral reason to unthrone them. Only the naïve and immature interpreter, therefore, dares to make collective

[9] Those who are acquainted with the history of science, or more specifically of medicine, have to admit, however, how often generally felt-for solutions found their counterpart in reality. Thus creative construction may be more than conventional. It seems altogether likely that future investigations will uncover a strong positive relation between creative construction of thought forms relevant to current knowledge and reality itself.

31

experience the starting point for critical and mature interpretation of Christ.

Yet this is often done, even by recognized thinkers. Such theological reflection is not rooted in reality but is rather an expression of defensive rationalization. It is ideology. It is the finding reasons by devotees for convictions already fixed. These reasons usually are defended by the assertions of half-truths, namely, (1) that individually and collectively we cannot escape from our own experience; and (2) that without commitment to such a judging truth as Christ we cannot help being unbelieving or rebellious, thus distorting the truth. When Christology, however, becomes mostly the telling to itself its own reasons for believing what it does, and involves no deeper confrontation with Christ Himself, it becomes the interpretation of Christian interpretation and not the interpretation of the Christ. Altogether too much theology is dependent not only upon secondhand experience but upon secondhand insight. Too much theology is in fact traditionalism regurgitated for the sake of giving security to those with no experience and for the sake of the acceptance of the theologian within the confines of a self-adulating community. Christ and ideology must not be equated.

On this point, however, we have to be exceedingly careful, for if no merely objective investigation is possible and if there is no presuppositionless reason, how can we get to Christ? Must we not land either in futile speculation or in a sterile dealing with facts that neither condemn nor save? In either case we are *not* practicing Christology. Hardy has pointedly reminded us that Athanasius' *On the Incarnation of the Word* "is not so much an exercise in the speculative reason as an appeal for personal decision." [10] Perhaps if we remember that the cause of Christ was the world and resolve in the depths of our hearts to live and to think his cause, we shall find the concern for others that will lead us out from the falsifications and defenses of the self to the land of true seeing. If we also bear deep in our lives the fact that the Holy Spirit whom Christ came to give is the Spirit of Truth, we shall openly invite the integrity of person and work that can never take personal or collective experience as the focal starting point for theological method, particularly for Christology. We shall rather become willing to find the focus in Christ himself where such experience is judged, illumined, cleansed and saved.

II. DO WE THEN START WITH HISTORY?

An obvious place to begin the study of Christ seems to be the Bible. In it we have the only record of the Christ of the Christian faith. Can we learn any real facts about the actual Christ who came in history apart from the only historical record we have? Should not our theology of Christ, therefore, be biblical theology?

For such a position at least three things can be said. In the first place, as we have intimated, here alone do we have the record of the primary facts. Any Christology that hopes to go beyond personal and collective experience to have these

[10] *Christology of the Late Fathers*, p. 45.

corrected by the facts ought therefore to come to the Bible, the supreme repository of these facts. In the second place, the experiences and interpretations of the original Christian community are to be found in the Bible. Thus history and experience come together in the Bible; the history of the Christ and of His community merge in the biblical record. Revelation through events is both attested to and recorded for us through the faith of the first Christian community; and the record is the Bible. In the third place, there is the practical consideration that all denominations or Christian groups alike use the Bible. These groups, too, because of the way we human beings bow to what is written, can best be led in terms of the Bible. Should not, therefore, the writer of Christology begin both logically and practically by taking the Bible in its natural sense and simply say of Jesus what the Bible tells us? Unfortunately the problem is not that simple, and fortunately, as we shall see, such is not the right answer. This much we can say now: If in the end we violate the heart of the Bible, we must fail; at the same time, not to start with the Bible is neither to slight it nor to disregard it.

There are two main reasons why the approach to any adequate Christology cannot be as simple as merely giving the biblical account. The first is that the implications of the biblical faith have been drawn out and welded into dogma or doctrines by generations and the centuries. Christian theology has developed far from its starting point in the biblical record. Theology is now advanced to the point where when we read our Bibles, we read them with centuries of theological interpretation in the back of our minds. We read the Bible *through the theology* we hold. Therefore different people find different things staring them in the face as they read, while others skip the same passages without seeing any special importance in them. On the subject of Christology it is amazing to see what a different picture of the Christ people get from their reading, even those who live day by day with the Bible. Sometimes such divergence is due to personality and character differences. Pfister has ventured to suggest in *Christianity and Fear* that he can tell what kind of person he is dealing with by the way that person interprets the Bible. His statement points up one truth. But more basically the difference of seeing is due to the total theological context and background that are presupposed. Our problem is, therefore, to cut not only deeper than the experience we now have individually and collectively but even deeper than the way we now read the Bible.

History helps at this point. A man who does not read history, or is ignorant of it, is like a man suffering from amnesia, or from a loss of memory. He can see, read, choose, but he does not know who he is, how he got to be what he is, and what the fuller meaning of his experience is. His experience is thin and flat rather than rich and deep. By the careful reading of history we can at least learn, if we are willing, how our theologians came to be what they are. We can see why and how the different interpretations came to be accepted or rejected and why some persisted even after being officially rejected. The Christian faith becomes adumbrated, amplified, enriched by being lived through the long and wide stretches of history. By being fought over, within and without, the faith becomes understood in its deeper implications for life and doctrine. Therefore the history of Christology should be studied.

Of books on Christ there is no practical end, for there is an abundance of introductory material.[11] The important consideration, however, is that anyone who wants to deal with Christology, in any developed and mature sense, ought to have mastered some historical facts rather carefully. History is a way to freedom from present fact. History is a way to discover as false what to us now may seem essential and to find as basic some facts and insights which we now disregard. Biblical theology needs to be studied in the light of historical theology. The Fathers always surprise us not only by their depth but by their modernity. Eternal truth is always relevant, especially if we penetrate below its historical form. If we can keep from making the Fathers authorities and learn from them without learning *them,* we shall be helped at the beginning of Christological inquiry. If history is used in this way it becomes an aid to the study of Christ; but if

[11] On the subject of Christ some knowledge of history is of utmost importance. Those who have any chance at all ought to read the *Ante-Nicene* and the *Nicene and Post-Nicene Fathers* or the *Library of Christian Classics,* particularly Vols. I and III. Others will want to read some history like Duchesne, *The Early History of the Church,* in three volumes. A most important single volume is R. V. Sellers, *The Council of Chalcedon,* or even his smaller *Two Ancient Christologies.* A truly insightful book is also Prestige, *Fathers and Heretics.* A short analytical summary is found in D. M. Baillie's *God Was in Christ,* but its importance far outweighs its brevity.

history is used as the textbook of the true development of Christology by the Church, care must be taken not to obscure the primitive Christologies of the New Testament itself. The study of both the biblical record and the historical development is needed in the theological quest for adequate Christology. History has both advanced our understanding of Christ and hidden him behind unreal theological constructions. We need, therefore, to study the Bible in the light of history and history in the light of the Bible.

The second main difficulty with making the Bible the decisive source for Christology is that no one faith is given in it. If the Bible were a lucid textbook or a well-developed philosophical argument instead of a living witness to the living Word of God, we should not have much trouble in beginning simply with the Bible. The Bible does contain much objective, propositional truth. The central truths of the Bible are literally correct: for example, God is Love and was in Christ reconciling the world unto Himself. Therefore Barth's contention that the Bible becomes the Word of God *only* for faith is too deeply tinged with subjectivism to speak the full truth. Nevertheless there is no one Christology given in the Bible. We have to choose, and can choose rightly, only when we encounter the living Word who inspired it; but such choice, as we shall see, is not independent of solid preparation both of study and of devotion.

It is hard to say how many different kinds of Christology are stated or implied by the New Testament. Our only point here is to show that there are more than one. We shall mention five kinds merely as examples.

1. Jesus was the Messiah. He was a man "who went about doing good." "God anointed Jesus of Nazareth with the Holy Spirit and with power . . . for God was with him" (Acts 10:38). God made him the Messiah, proving his appointment particularly by the Resurrection from the dead. Primitive Christology tells Jesus of Nazareth as "a man attested to by God" (Acts 2:22). Much of the material in the Synoptic Gospels and in the Acts of the Apostles develops this theme. The Early Church of Jerusalem espoused this view to the point where there had to be a major Council at Jerusalem in 49 A.D. to decide that the Gospel was also for the Gentiles.[12]

2. Jesus was God. Although such a crass statement as to the stature of Jesus seems quite alien to Jewish thought and is difficult to find in any unqualified, developed sense in the New Testament, particularly if all the passages in any book are taken into account, nevertheless Thomas called him "my God," and the Book of Revelation ascribes honors to him, at least devotionally, as "King of Kings" and "Lord of Lords." In the Epistle to the Colossians we find the claim that "in him the fullness of God was pleased to dwell (Col. 1:19). And "in him dwells the whole fullness of deity bodily" (Col. 2:29). Even though we may not legitimately press such statements far enough to say simply "Jesus was

[12] Cf. Acts 15.

God," [13] there seems to be a strand in the New Testament that pulls toward this position.

3. Jesus was the *Logos*. In the beginning was this *Logos*, with and of God, through whom all things were made and all men enlightened. This *Logos* of God, who is God, became personally present in Jesus in the fullness of time, full of grace and truth, to the point that we see the very glory of God in the face of Jesus Christ. This *Logos* is the outgoing Godhood in creative and communicative relations. The Gospel according to St. John, by not using the definite article in the Greek before God, makes "God" adjectival, the eternally divine Word.

4. Jesus was the first-born among many creatures or of all creation. Even if the Greek middle voice would make the meaning of Colossians 1:15 "creating," the side that Jesus is on is that of creation, not of the Creator. Christ is then a creature, the first-born and the pre-eminent, through whom all things are made and through whom all things are saved. Technically, such passages as these gave much comfort and hot ammunition to the Arians in their long struggle to have Jesus understood as made in the image and likeness of God rather than as very God of very God.

5. Jesus was the adopted Son of God.[14] The Letter to

[13] Such an outstanding authority on biblical and historical theology as Principal Nathaniel Micklem calls the assertion, "Jesus is God," a "shocking heresy" (*Ultimate Questions*, p. 131).

[14] "But here there is a curious contradiction. If Jesus *is* God he cannot be 'exalted' to be God. He is already exalted by nature of his Godhead. Yet the New Testament does not teach this at all. It teaches that Jesus was exalted to be Lord, not *Theos* but *Kyrios*" (Geraint Vaughan Jones, *Christology and Myth in the New Testament*, p. 146).

the Hebrews, for one example, has the Son becoming superior to angels on hearing God's "Today I have begotten thee" (1:4-5). A passage like Philippians 2:5-8 (where God gave Jesus a name above all names because of his humility in not thinking equality with God a thing to be snatched at but going instead all the way to a shameful death) is another interesting illustration of one kind of primitive Christology that is for a large part Adoptionist. (The kenotic aspect, however, must not be neglected!) G. V. Jones goes so far as to write: "This early kerygma knows nothing of an incarnational Christology, for the Messiah was not conceived of incarnationally. The *kerygma* was, if anything, vaguely Adoptionist; yet it was the Johannine doctrine which became normative for theology." [15]

If it had not been for these varying Christologies in the Bible there would have been no need for many Councils to interpret the central meaning of the Bible. Those who disagreed with the main tradition were not merely obstinate or foolish men. They were far from ignorant or unlearned. They were men who had fastened on a few verses in the Bible as the only or main biblical position and were willing to suffer and to be condemned by men because they were sure they were right with God and would be vindicated by history. They sincerely believed themselves to be biblical and were backed by some biblical strands.

The Bible, however, witnesses only to the foundational events of Christology, to what Bishop Aulén has called "the

[15] *Ibid.,* p. 61.

Christ-deed." The Bible expresses the authoritative meaning
of Christ; and, therefore, any and every Christology must
prove itself biblical in the best sense of that word, if it is
to command the respect of Christians and be rightly called
Christian. There is no short-cut, however, to the discovery
of what is central to the Bible, even in Christology. When we
finally discover the way to Christ and to his authority we
shall find that it requires the whole man in devotion, study
and service. The Bible is not a collection of doctrines but
a living Light in which to know and to walk. We, therefore,
grant the primacy of the Bible as objective standard, but
not in the sense that its truth can be taken by violence without
careful preparation and open pursuit. When the truth of
Christ in the Bible finally shines on us, free of all interfer-
ences of experience and historic dogma, we shall find that
experience itself becomes fulfilled while the Bible itself becomes interpreted through Christ in a new fullness and
power. God's truth alone can set the Bible free for us—the
truth of His Agape in Jesus Christ.

If, then, we need to study history in order to understand
how we have come to our present Christologies as well as
to become clear on the point that the Bible offers us the
risk and the glory of choice and study, can we not find an
adequate starting place merely by continuing history from
the Bible on, to find out what the great ecumenical councils
had to say? What are the basic historic affirmations of Christology and how do they satisfy or fail to satisfy our need
for an adequate point of departure in the study of Christ?

41

There are two summary statements we have to make on this point: (1) What the Councils actually said at the heart of Christology and (2) the nature of the Councils themselves.

There are, I believe, four basic Ecumenical Councils dealing with the heart of Christology: Nicaea, 325, considering the relation of Christ to God; Constantinople, 381, taking up the relation of Christ to man; Chalcedon, 451, affirming the unity of Jesus' personality with respect to both God and man; and the Sixth Ecumenical Council (Third Council of Constantinople), 681, declaring the perpetual distinction between the two natures and their separate fullness. Each of these makes an affirmation basic to Christian faith.

Nicaea settled the question of the full deity of Jesus. He who came in Jesus was no secondary God and no cosmic creature, but the one and only God, creator and lord of the universe. He who himself and alone defines and constitutes eternity was truly and literally present in Jesus as the fullness of time. Time became fulfilled by eternity when man became *fulfilled* by God. The distinction between *homoousios* and *homoiousios* (of the same nature or of similar nature) may seem less than essential, and yet no question can be more decisive. Nicaea affirmed that Jesus was, not *like,* but *of* God. That being so, we have seen in human history and in human life *God's very nature,* or God Himself truly present. To say that we know God only in His acts, as the Reformers tend to do, as is also the approach of some modern theologians like Barth, is to deny Nicaea at its core. It is not merely a question here, between an active and a static view of God. The issue is not whether God reveals Himself through a noun or through a verb, through being or through doing. Nicaea held the indispensable minimum of any adequate Christology to be that in Jesus as the Christ we have truly seen, met and been made to decide concerning God Himself. Nicaea is the bedrock affirmation that in Jesus Christ we meet the only, true and full deity. With Nicaea we affirm that in some ultimate sense God Himself came, acted and saved us in Jesus Christ.

The First Council of Constantinople settled the question of the full humanity of Jesus. He was a man among men, in no constitutive way different from any man. The deity of Jesus was not due to any subtraction from his humanity. Such sinlessness as was exhibited was fulfillment of human nature or maturity, a continually decisive depth-response to the will of God within and without. Apollinaris in his deep and beautiful devotion to his Savior had wanted him at some crucial point unique, essentially different from all human beings as human beings. Since to Apollinaris *nous,* or mind, was the constitutive element of humanity, Jesus must at least have had deity for mind. Soul and body could be human, he felt, but not the center of Jesus' personality. *Nous* was also the seat of human freedom and Apollinaris believed that Jesus, being God, could not even be free to sin. The center of Jesus' personality must consequently have been the Second Person of the Trinity, the Word who became flesh, the eternal Son of the Father. Thus spoke deep devotion against the Antiochian stress on the humanity of Jesus which to Apollinaris seemed to make Jesus a Spirit-filled man. This devout man craved God to worship in Jesus and he could not feel that he was really worshiping God if Jesus was also fully and in all respects human. For Apollinaris Jesus had in some sense to be God *or* man, never fully God *and* man. The Ecumenical Council, however, in its deep wisdom and high inspiration, said a definite and final "no" to Apollinaris. Jesus was in all respects truly and and fully human, as human as we. Right Christology is never subtraction at any point from our full humanity. Jesus was, not *like,* but *of* man. He was not *homoiousios,* but *homoousios* with us.

Actually we cannot be truly historical, of course, without recognizing that the Fathers had undermined the formula of Chalcedon before it was written by holding that a self-contained Personal Being, the Second Person in the Trinity, had come down and assumed impersonal human nature in Jesus Christ.[16] Especially beginning with Athanasius and Cyril we have a line of thought that equates the divine Second Person of the Trinity with the ego of Jesus. Jesus, therefore, is eternal, was sovereignly present in the cradle, and only apparently grew in wisdom and stature. What this position actually holds is the Personal God and an impersonal humanity united, not God and man, both fully personal, organically united. Later on, with the Calvinist theologians especially, we get little or no stress on the view in the Incarnation of two integral realities, God and man, but instead we find the eternal Son taking on impersonal humanity as

[16] For a fuller discussion of this point see chap. 2.

a vehicle through which to communicate. That Chalcedon is right in its formulation, however, is the underlying theme of our analysis. This being so, we can arrive at a whole new theology, metaphysics and personal faith when we take with all seriousness the seemingly preposterous claim that in Jesus Christ we have the Godman who is truly consubstantial with God and with man.

Chalcedon, furthermore, settled the question of the unity of Jesus' personality. He was the Son of God and the Son of Man in the expressive as well as the representative meaning of the terms, and yet he was also one true historical personality like ourselves. *Both Sons were present at once in him and yet Jesus was not two sons but one.* The two natures of God and man, each fully personal, were truly present, without any diminution or confusion of essential being, and yet the personality of Jesus that ensued was more united, integrated, and real than any personality that is less God and less man. To keep them apart, even in emphasis, was the heresy of which Nestorius was accused and for which, with whatever justification, he was condemned. To merge them into one, on the other hand, in such a way that either nature ceases to be or is absorbed into the other was the heresy of the Monophysites, those who believed, like Severus, that out of two natures came one. The Christ never was nor became of one nature, either with God or with man, but rather, being consubstantial with both God and man, became the Godman, the Christ, expressing not only the eternal purpose of the Father before the creation of the world but also the full historic purpose of man since the beginning of creation and up to the ending of human time. The two natures in Christ, according to Chalcedon, were "without confusion, without change, without division, without separation" and "in one Person." This formula is not archaic but the best guide to a true Christology that can be genuine for us now.

The Sixth Ecumenical Council settled the question of the permanence of the two natures within one personality. It would not grant "one natural operation of God and the creature, lest we should either raise up into the divine nature what is created, or bring down the pre-eminence of the divine nature into the place suitable for things that are made." [17] The specific reason for the Council was the Monothelite controversy, in which some claimed that even if Jesus did not have a divine ego, as decided by Constantinople, at least he did not have any will of his own, but had only God's will. The Council, even at this late date, refused to countenance so great a heresy as this and to destroy in doctrine the full and integral humanity of Jesus. It is astounding to a historian of doctrine, knowing the irrational flood-power of well-meaning devotion, that the worship of Jesus had not at this time so undermined the stress on his real humanity that the Council could affirm the metaphysical distinction of God's will and Jesus' will. Although the Council is weak on the

[17] Hardy, *op. cit.*, p. 384.

functional understanding of the need for the human will to operate with some independence and feeble as to the New Testament's plain insistence on the operation of the human will of Jesus in actual, conscious contradistinction to God's,[18] it nailed down the fact that never can the human be lifted into Godhood or the Godhood lowered into humanity. Therefore the Council said with unmistakable clarity that the humanity of Jesus always remained inviolably human. Thus, in effect, Incarnation means boldly and consistently that Jesus was and is forever consubstantial with God and with man. In other words, the main decisions of the major Councils are clear on the point that theophany, the coming of God into a human body without full human nature, is heresy; whereas orthodoxy centers undeniably in Incarnation, the fullness of God in the fullness of man in the fullness of time. No interpretation that falls short of accepting the oneness of God, the oneness of Jesus, and the fullness of both natures in Jesus can ever be completely Christian. By these standards shall all true interpreters judge every Christology.

If in the best knowledge and fullest competence anyone should believe that the Councils are wrong at their heart and affirm a truth and a faith adequate for a new day and of fuller understanding with the religions of the world, he should be honest at this point and state either that he has given up historic Christianity in its main contentions that

18 Cf., for instance, "not my will, but thine, be done," in Luke 22:42.

Jesus is the Christ, or else that he has found a glorious, liberating truth so great and so precious that the original message of the Christian faith can itself, when more truly understood and accepted, set straight the Dogmatic Councils. For my part, however, the center of my understanding is that in the mystery of the full relation of God to man in Jesus as the Christ lies the heart of truth, for modern man as well as for men of all ages. We shall therefore go on building on the Bible and on the history of Christian thought, even though we cannot start here, for reasons that will be forthcoming more and more. The Councils give the positive pointers to correct Christology; our task is to show that with the right *content* of Christology we can follow their directions and fulfill their intentions while at the same time we can release Christology to become the creative center of the interpretation of human life and history in their relation to God.

We have now indicated concisely what is the main brunt of Christological assertions in the major Ecumenical Councils. It remains to suggest the nature of the Councils. They were creative events, dynamically charting the way of faith, not the promulgators of closed canons or creeds beyond reconsideration, reinterpretation and reformulation. The Ecumenical Councils made living decisions on live issues. Because one Council had discussed and settled an issue there was no thought that other Councils could not be called creatively to appraise new aspects of the original problem, to rescind what had been done, to ward off a new danger, or to stress a new facet of the findings. The Church acted and spoke through Councils which generally affirmed the previous Councils but were free to face anew the great issues of the faith. The Councils were authoritative, not authoritarian; they were creative, not limiting events.

My conviction is that the major Councils aimed at, and usually arrived at, at least formally, the center of the Christian truth. Therefore every responsible Christian thinker, especially every leader of Christian thought, ought to listen long and well to what the voice of Ecumenical Christianity has proclaimed. To differ from the historic Christian position ought to involve much pain and self-examination before God in prayer, constant, open study, rigorous self-discipline, surrender of one's own will—even one's will to integrity to whatever extent such a will may be a screen for self-importance or deep-level rebellion. But even as the Christ came in the weakness of the flesh, incognito, that we through him might find our own faith, even as the Bible is the holy Word of God within the ambiguous words of men, and even as the Church is the very presence of God within the fallibilities of men, even so the Councils express basic truths concerning God's coming to man and in man, although necessarily within a mixture of historic circumstance and human ignorance, and with some admixture of political and personal self-seeking. The heart of the Councils in their major decisions, I believe, is sound, at least for what they say formally; but the Councils are not to be worshiped but *used,* that we, too, in our times may come to have creative Councils, warding off current dangers to the faith and charting new ways of interpreting the eternal truth of God's presence in Christ for our salvation.[19]

We must also remember realistically that the Councils made mistakes. Not only were some mistakes repudiated by succeeding Councils but also some have not yet been rectified. Such a decision, for instance, as the condemnation of Origen for believing in God's ultimate victory over all sin, death and law, and the final restoration in eternity of all things that God might be all in all, has not so far been repudiated by any Ecumenical Council. If the foundation of the Christian faith be truly Christ, and if the Sovereign Lord is saving Love, such a condemnation was not only a major mistake but even a tragedy for the Christian church. Nor has any Council guarded explicitly and sufficiently against the treacherous and lethal doctrine of the "impersonal humanity" of Jesus, whereby he was in effect declared not a man but only man in general. As we shall see at length, this stress is in effect docetism, the denial of the real humanity of Jesus, couched in so subtle and appealing a form that it is hard to realize that this doctrine is a deathblow to any adequate doctrine of the Incarnation.

While the Councils made doctrine more precise they also

---

[19] From a Christian perspective, as we shall see, the silence of the Councils on the main truth of the Christian faith, God as Agape, is astounding!

narrowed their theological base in comparison with the full New Testament data. A learned Jesuit divine, Father Petevius, showed in the seventeenth century that the theologians of the first three centuries used with natural ease phrases and statements which since then have been designated as heretical. If the New Testament were published today, for the first time, it would never pass the censorship of any orthodox Christian group inasmuch as its several strands over the ages have been debated, some lifted to correct doctrine while others have been relegated to unconscious, practical deletion. We have needed the Councils. We need to check their findings, however, with the New Testament just as we need to check the New Testament itself with its own governing center.

Is this center of the New Testament, however, available to us apart from the decision of the Councils? Can we go behind the Councils to the original Gospel? Can we distinguish between the eternal Gospel, testified to at its center by the Councils, and the time-bound form of man's thinking, adding to, subtracting from, or changing the stress of the Gospel itself? Upon this distinction hangs the whole question of authority in the Christian faith. It involves a decision which modern man must make. Bultmann in Europe and Tillich in the United States have opened up the problem at its center and at some depth; it can no longer be ignored. How can we escape, to use the thought of Peter Taylor Forsyth, from divorcing the witness of the Spirit from the witness of the Word, if we truly and confidently welcome and heed the witness of the Spirit? [20] We shall soon begin to grapple with this central task. In the meantime we should not leave the question of the historical, whether of the Bible or of church history, without reminding ourselves of the basic truth that Christian confession, the heart of the creeds, is best carried on not by argument but by worship. When the Bible and creeds become enveloped with prayer and praise, they will serve not the mind puffed up by knowledge, but the love that truly builds up the body of Christ. Christology must rise out of doxology, but a doxology of the whole man, including integrity and competence of scholarship and creative thought.

III. WE START WITH CHRIST AS AGAPE

If for theological method on the subject of Christ we can start neither with experience nor with the historical as such, where then can we find the most adequate beginning? We suggest that Christ himself is the best place to start. Obvi-

[20] Or can the Word be separated from the words of the Bible, the *logos* from the *lalia?* If we thus peel the onion, so to speak, do we in fact infringe the incarnational principle of the hypostatic union? Lionel Thornton claims that we cannot cull out a strand of truth without destroying the unity of the Incarnation: "Scripture as a whole is that Whole with which Revelation is to be identified" (*Revelation and the Modern World,* p. 130). Thomas Torrance has claimed, however, that the "Holy Scripture belongs to the sphere where redemption is necessary. The Bible stands above the Church, speaking to the Church the very Word of God, but the Bible also belongs to history which comes under the judgment and the redemption of the Cross" (*Essays in Christology in Honor of Karl Barth,* T. H. L. Parker, ed. p. 25). If this is true how can we understand the double function of the Bible, without infringing the incarnational principle of the Word? What constitutes a fully Christian biblical stardard? This point we must spell out before we end this chapter.

ously such a starting place seems desirable and would be chosen by many if the problem were that easy. The question remains, nevertheless, how can we start with Christ without beginning either with our experience of him or with what the Bible or history as such tell of him? There is the rub! The truth and importance of this volume in large measure depends upon it. For this reason we must answer this decisive query with equally decisive clarity. In any case, the claim that our theology is centrally Christian depends upon the answer. If the starting point is correct and meaningful, we have both the right and the need for basic theological revision in order to let the Christian faith become rightly understood and properly effective. If this starting point is wrong, on the other hand, our whole theology needs redoing. In such a case, at least, this theology should be declared to be a God-centered interpretation within the context of God as holy Love, even if it is not an authentic spokesman for historic Christianity. For even as Jesus and Paul both thought of themselves as within Judaism and yet founded Christianity; and even as John Wesley considered himself an Anglican but had in effect moved away from the central drives of his old allegiance, so it could be that our position aims at the universal truth of God as Agape whereas historic Christianity is in effect a sectarian confession. The reason we believe, nevertheless, that what is centrally Christian historically is also final, universal truth, is precisely that our starting point in Christ and the theology of God as Agape coincide. What then is this starting point? Just how is

starting with Christ decisively different from other possible
points of departure that we have discussed? Even though
we shall devote the remainder of the chapter to a detailed
consideration of this topic, a summary paragraph at this
point may be helpful in giving proper perspective.

We start with Jesus Christ himself as Agape, the Event-
Meaning that most fully explains our experience and our
world, most severely reveals and judges our sins and our
failures, and most fully offers final salvation. Such a start
cannot be made in our experience *as such* or in the Bible
or history *as such*. Even so, we commence at this point
because Jesus Christ as Agape both illumines experience
as no other reality does and also most fully enables us to
understand what is biblical. We begin, furthermore, with
Jesus Christ as Agape because by so doing we are employing
the distinctive and determinative motif of the Christian
faith, and therefore, the key to the understanding of the
Church and the history of its theology. We start with Jesus
Christ, with Agape, as *Event-Meaning* because Jesus Christ
is the personal Event that yields the conclusive meaning for
the theological context of the Christian faith. He is a Person
who must be encountered as a historic Event, but that Event
affords us meaning not only for communication of the Event,
but the Meaning of meanings, or the total context for the
ultimate interpretation of our experience, history and world
process. We are, therefore, dealing with a pattern of Christ,
"a picture," as Tillich might say, that organizes, explains
and offers fulfillment for all other patterns of truth. We

start with Christ as Truth, the living Truth, who is both irreducibly personal and yet provides us the context for ultimate thinking, the master context for life and thought. Reason needs *right fact, right reasoning* and *right context.* Christ as Agape, the Event-Meaning, while beyond the context of general experience, demanding the decision of encounter, is nevertheless accessible to fact and reasoning. In starting with the selective most high of history, rather than with general experience and its interpretation, we are, indeed, observing the requirements of an adequate theological method, as demonstrated in *Faith and Reason.* The Event affords us the co-ordinating context for all other events.[21]

There are several points that should be clarified if we are to have any right to say that in beginning our Christology with Christ as Agape, the Event-Meaning of God's Christ-deed, we are not starting with either experience or history as such, but with the Truth within experience and history that most fully explains and fulfills both. The points to be clarified in particular are the following: Christ and the Jesus of history, Christ and the Bible, Christ and the creeds, and Christ and method or truth in general.

The relation between Christ and the Jesus of history constitutes a complicated problem. In general, the contemporary scholarly opinion is that we can know little about the historic Jesus. This opinion is based partly on the nature

[21] Excellent reasoning along these lines has been done for us by Dorothy Emmet in *The Nature of Metaphysical Thinking.*

of historical knowledge in general and partly on the lack
of a consistent picture of the historic Jesus. It is also in some
measure originated in and intensely reinforced by the theological presupposition of Kierkegaard that eternity and time
are qualitatively distinct and that therefore we can learn
nothing from history about the revelation of the Absolute.
The relative, Kierkegaard assumes, cannot contain the Absolute; and therefore from history we learn nothing about
Jesus Christ. Indeed, as we have already quoted him, "knowledge demolishes Jesus Christ." Great theologians like Barth
and Tillich, and New Testament scholars like Bultmann,
have been greatly influenced by this philosophical presupposition. Nevertheless, beyond such influence of Kierkegaard,
the fact remains that to reconstruct any full and detailed
life of the historic Jesus is most difficult.[22]

Apart from general skepticism, however, we can establish
the general nature of the life of Jesus, the basic nature of
his teachings, and the outcome of his historic life. The life of
Jesus, from the beginning of its mission to its end, seems to
have been one of Agape. If we proceed from his willingness
to enter into the baptism for the remission of sin, his tempta-

---

[22] In a real sense we appreciate the emphasis of Bultmann to this effect:
"How he actually originated matters little, indeed we can appreciate his
significance only when we cease to worry about such questions" ("New Testament and Mythology" in Bartsch, *Kerygma and Myth,* p. 35). We differ with
Bultmann, however, in understanding that the historic Event, no matter
what the details of its origin, if it is the central starting point involves an
organismic interpretation of experience that requires, from within itself, the
construction of a metaphysics or of a total theological context, that utilizes
reason at its critical and creative best. In his *Essays, Philosophical and Theological* Bultmann has, in fact, dismissed such a context as Stoicism's impor-
tation of *Weltanschauung* within the developing Christian faith.

tions in the wilderness, his healings, and his being hated for teachings concerning the love of God that undermined external rules and teachings, and continue through his washing of his disciples' feet, his total surrender to death in Gethsemane and his praying for those who crucified him, we get a general picture or pattern of God's love, taught and lived. A more careful examination of his parables and teachings discloses that the central motif within them is Agape. The final result is a reliable, general picture that is dependent upon neither any details of apostolic witness nor any fanciful *ipsissima verba*. The apostolic witness may misinterpret at points and we know no certain "very words of Jesus," but we have undeniably an overall commanding pattern of Jesus' teaching of Agape. The deepest reason for his being killed, in fact, was that he claimed to be the Son of God, an abhorrent God of Agape whose very perfection involved indiscriminate kindness to all, as illustrated by his giving rain to both the just and the unjust. Further, God put His approval on this life of Agape by raising him from the dead. Whatever historical form this event may have taken, it was God's saying Yes to Jesus, in Bultmann's terms; history confirmed his life by changing the calendar after him; and he became the center of a movement even now spreading to the ends of the earth. Whatever details of Jesus' life and teachings may or may not be true, the historical fact stands that there once lived a man, Jesus, who so lived and taught God as Agape that human history came to a fulfillment of all previous approaches to such an understanding of God, transforming and correcting them, as well as fulfilling them. Jesus thus put into the world the pattern of God as Agape.

Now we are beginning to see how we can start with Christ himself as a historical figure, but not with history as such or with the historical Jesus as such. The approach, to be sure, is through history, for Jesus was in history, but only through the truth of eternity in history. We start with Christ only because in history we have found one who by his living and teaching affords us the ultimate context for interpreting life and cosmic process, and who, as we shall see, goes beyond both life and process as such only because God was at the center of his being and teaching. Such is, in fact, the truth of the Incarnation. The Incarnation is found in history, but the center of its reality is never humanity or human history. Thus in starting with this pattern of Jesus Christ as Agape, the Event-Meaning, we have a historical approach that is nevertheless free of the detailed problems of the historical Jesus and that will eventuate in a different kind of theology from that which makes the historical Jesus central. Although we cannot know the historic Jesus, then, we can know the historic Christ.

Next we consider Christ and the Bible. Agape as God's Christ-deed is the Event-Meaning that is both the distinctive and determinative motif of the Christian faith and also the culminating climax and organizing center of the New Testament. Therefore this Event-Meaning is the summit of the Bible that when once seen is pointed to by its total message. Outside the Bible we have no record of Christ as Agape.

Ohm, in a thorough study of the motif of Christian love in other living religions, *Die Liebe zu Gott in den Nicht-Christlichen Religionen,* has found that neither in the Bhakti Marga of Hinduism,[23] nor in Mahayana Buddhism nor even in Amida Buddhism, is there another revelation of God as Agape, but only at most preparatory approaches. Such approaches to Agape are, of course, from God, even as St. Paul writes that God is the God of all religions, "of Gentiles also, since God is one"![24] The biblical message of God as Agape is nevertheless distinctive. At this point, however, we reaffirm our readiness, yes, even our eagerness, to find Agape in any place where it truly may have come, but after years of open and careful searching we must conclude that to the best of our knowledge Ohm's findings are correct.

The Agape *Grundmotif,* or basic, regulative pattern, is also determinative for the Bible.[25] The Old Testament, although having a message of its own and for its own time, is nevertheless fulfilled in the New. The Old Testament never has a personal embodiment or an explicit teacher of God as Agape. The limits of election and covenant love, to be sure, are overflowed in the best of Old Testament thought, as in Leviticus 19, Deutero-Isaiah, Hosea, Ruth, and Jonah, but nowhere is Agape made central both to cosmos (ultimate reality) and to conduct (personal and social life). Moffatt

[23] Consider Appasamy's interesting *Christianity as Bhakti Marga.*
[24] Rom. 3:29-30.
[25] I am reminded of Athenagoras' Plea: "The Son of God is the *mind* and Word of the Father" (Richardson, ed., *Early Christian Fathers,* p. 309). Protracted reading convinced me that the Fathers were tireless in stressing *meaning.*

has shown in *Love in the New Testament* how Love is central to the New Testament; and a larger, more detailed work is Victor Warnach's *Agape*. There are many who charge that Jesus never went beyond previous teachings. They cannot know what they are saying, for either they have never had their eyes opened to Agape as the central truth of the New Testament or else they have fought shy of such a frightening Love. When their eyes once are opened they can exult with Emil Brunner that the whole Bible is only a commentary on the one word, Agape, either negatively or positively!

Are we then saying that Agape is necessarily the most frequent and therefore the dominating motif? By no means! It is declared to be the greatest of all and is summarized in the self-giving and victorious Love on the Cross and in the Resurrection, but there are numerous lesser motifs and several contradictory ones even in the New Testament. Why are they there? It may be because Jesus himself, though at heart so much one with God that his interpretation of God and his teachings had to take on the context of Agape, was yet also so much one with his people and training that he never logically and fully cleansed his teachings of inconsistent elements. Such inconsistencies remain in the pioneers and perfectors of our faith; the Holy Spirit of truth must then lead their followers into fuller understanding of the revolutionary, all-demanding center of Truth. More likely, however, the disciples never fully understood Jesus, the less so the more novel and revolutionary was his teaching. The wonder is that his teachings and parables during the formative period of New Testament writing obtained and retained so much of Agape that this motif became the shaping reality of New Testament thought. We must remember, further- more, that the New Testament issues out of secondary witnesses well removed from the immediate deliverances of Jesus, reflecting, in large part, the life and attitudes of the Church. God never violates human personality and never forces dictation even on eyewitnesses. Oral tradition is suffi- ciently reliable to record an unmistakable historic person with a revolutionary teaching, but not foolproof enough to pre- vent inconsistent elements congenial to human nature to become part of its content.

There is another reason, however, why the Bible includes subagapaic elements. The function of the Bible, within the indirect purposiveness of God rather than within His direct purposefulness, is to illumine the whole of human experi- ence in the light of the consummating and saving reality and relation of Agape. The whole of human experience, black and gray and of many varied themes, needs the whole Bible to illumine and interpret its meaning, and to judge and save its content. When the whole of experience in the Bible is lifted up to Christ and lit by His presence as Agape, the whole of actual human experience can be shown up for what it is, for what is wrong with it, for what it means, and for what can become of it. In the light of the summit and controlling reality of the Bible, we can then use all subagapaic themes, being able to discriminate, for instance, between the attitude of Paul who was willing to be damned for the sake of his brothers, the Jews, and the saints in heaven in the Book of Revelation who cried day and night for revenge. The Bible is the mirror for our lives. It is impossible for us to turn back on ourselves and to see our own faces directly. We can see them only in mirrors or on pictures. Just so we cannot turn around and catch direct sight of our own spiritual countenance. But God has given us indirect ways of seeing ourselves, and the standard mirror for the human spirit is the Bible, when the whole of human experience in it is illumined by the light of Christ as holy Love. In the light of Jesus Christ we see both the glory of God and the grime and stains on our own faces. Therefore we need to accept the Bible realistically for its fallibilities and for its falsehoods as well as for its perfection. Only thus is the Bible allowed to serve its true function.

Should not Agape, however, be at least interpreted by the Bible? Should we not take the whole New Testament teaching and fill out the meaning of Agape in its terms? No; to do so is, in fact, to make the revelation of no effect, for it is to misunderstand both how the Bible was actually written and for what purpose it includes the subagapaic themes. Such an interpretation takes the edge off the sword of the Spirit, becomes a covert for the refusal to accept the full Christian message in thought and in life, and introduces or maintains all the confusion that keeps the faith from being effective. Agape is a self-sufficient and self-consistent standard, a meaning derived from a personal life and the basic teachings that sprang out of that life.

Agape is, first of all, always God-centered. God alone is the Source, Standard, Authority and Dynamic of Agape. Agape is therefore self-sufficient, not as Being in terms of which to interpret God but as God in terms of whom to interpret being. Agape is therefore not relational in the sense that it is dependent upon community. There is no need, in the sense of lack, in Agape as ultimate reality. Since Agape is thus God-centered, the Old Testament faith and the best in natural theology, such as in Romans 2, are presupposed.[26] We believe in God and also in Jesus Christ as Agape. The Old Testament faith in God as the living, personal Spirit is a prerequisite for the understanding of Agape.

Agape is also completely universal in its creative and redemptive concern. No wall or barrier can shut out relation to God who is Agape. Agape is, furthermore, unconditional love. Agape is never dependent upon the response of the object for its motivation. In Nygren's terms in his *Agape and Eros,* Agape is unconditional, uncaused, unmotivated, groundless, uncalculating, spontaneous Love, creative of fellowship. This pattern, moreover, is sovereignly self-consistent and refuses all compromises. Agape can *create* and *use* pedagogically both Eros (seeking love) and Philia (mutual

---

[26] Langdon Gilkey, in reading the first draft of the manuscript, warned against starting with Christ apart from the Old Testament and natural theology. He pointed out that in our churches the great danger to Christology is a sentimental and unhistorical "Jesus cult." Even though we *start* with the incarnate Word of the historic Christ, we shall show how such a start cannot ever end in a "Jesus cult" if the method is adequate and competently pursued.

love), but in the end the nature of God is Agape (self-sufficient Love), completely outgoing and self-giving, as witnessed by God's going to death on the Cross, not for friends, but for sinners. Love for enemies, if need be, is an intrinsic, inseparable part of Agape, universally, unconditionally and eternally. Such is the heart of the biblical faith which is denied when Agape is watered down and made ineffective by attempts to define it indiscriminately in terms of the low as well as the high level of meaning in the New Testament. Such endeavors are doubly wrong: they sin both against God's Christ who alone is the Lord of the Bible and also against the very function and purpose of the Bible itself.

It should now be clear why with regard to method for Christology we start not with the Bible *as such,* but with Christ as the pattern of truth, the personal Spirit who is Agape, just as we start not with the historical Jesus in any detailed sense, but with the Agape pattern that is the Spirit, Jesus known in his revealing of the Presence of God and therefore known no longer according to the flesh.

Our next topic is Christ and the creeds. Positively, the creeds give the externally right requirements for Christology: one God, truly God, truly man, in one personality. The Christian faith is and remains monotheistic. Any interpretation of Christ that leads to polytheism is wrong. In Jesus we have seen God truly and in him God has worked His mighty Christ-deed in history. In Jesus we have also seen true man, both in respect to his becoming man and to his being the flowering of manhood. Jesus was not some being who was more than human personality at its best nor less than human personality, but a personality that was made up of God's presence and man's in such organic and fulfilling togetherness as to be the kind of human personality that God intended, in the first place, by the creation of man, and such an intrinsic and inviolate involvement of God that apart from Him this personality could not be. Thus the creeds, in affirming one God, *of* God, not like God, *of* man, not like man, in one true personality, give the right positive pointers for Christology.

Negatively, on the contrary, the creeds are not Christian. They are not Christian, in the first place, because they do not mention, let alone center in, the God who is Agape. The distinctive and determinative motif of the Christian faith cannot be found in the creeds of Christendom. The eternal God became man to show us His heart and to give us His help. Divine power spoke in human history in the Christ. The New Testament still moves with the presence and power of the Christian center. The Fathers contain much of this Christian center of Agape in their writings. It may be, however, that God's searching and saving Presence was too dreadful a reality for the Church; and that therefore institutionalized men like those who once crucified the God of glory to put a stop to His judging Agape, subconsciously crucified Him anew in the creeds. The creeds are repeated and loved in large measure as the affirmation of the shell of the faith that can keep in, and thus shut away, the content of Christ. So subtle are fear and rebellion, and mixed with what is good and true, that they make use of the language of orthodoxy to prevent the true faith from becoming clear and cleansing.

Negatively, in the second place, the creeds are not Christian because they fail to release the full sense and meaning of Jesus Christ as the historic unveiling of the co-presence of God and man. In Jesus man becomes true man and fulfills the intention of God in creating man. Somehow the creeds increasingly assumed in Jesus a divine Ego and a human material. The full meaning of Jesus' human personality as a human being among other human beings is not made clear and important in the creeds. God became the personal part of the equation; man, the impersonal. Jesus became Man, and not *a* man; whereas, in history, the Son of Man was a man who was also Son of God. The creeds kept Jesus Christ from being real and relevant by making him into a myth of sentimental devotion, rather than the center of history and of man in his proper relation to God. God's relevance in him for all other human beings is both neglected and obscured. Therefore, whenever we become ready to take seriously the positive criteria of the creeds—one God, *of* God and *of* man—and follow through in our interpretation, we shall be more right and more Christian than when we take the history of theology on its negative side as it effectively denies increasingly the co-presence of God and man in one historic personality. For these reasons, in spite of the positive correctness of the creeds with regard to the composition of

Christology, we should not start with the creeds as such but with the Christ who in actual fact has already fulfilled them.

This Event-Meaning of Jesus Christ as the presence, pattern and power of God enmanned should also be examined in relation to method. The method as outlined in *Faith and Reason* required a dynamic synthesis of faith and reason. Part of this synthesis is objective; part of it is subjective.

Objectively, Jesus Christ as Agape is the pattern that affords the maximum of explanatory meaning. On the objective side of the picture Agape is the locus of solution for our intellectual and practical problems. This method, we repeat, involves three tests: *right fact, right reasoning* and *right context.* We are confident that there is no real rival to God's Christ-deed, His own incoming as Agape, to explain why we are here, what we can do about it, and what is the meaning and reality of our eventual destiny.[27] In Christ all things do hang together. He is the center not only of history but of meaning. He is Event beyond meaning, yet also the context for ultimate meaning. He is of history, and the largest and most significant frame for history, and yet before, beyond and after all earthly history.

This objective context, however, must necessarily, by the nature of the case, be also subjective. The objective aspects of Jesus Christ as the Event-Meaning of Agape require their subjective counterparts. First of all, the pattern of Christ is subjective because it originates for us in the historical.

[27] Cf. the author's *The Christian Fellowship, The Christian Faith and Higher Education,* and especially *Faith and Reason, Evil and the Christian Faith, Christianity and Society,* and *The Christian Understanding of God.*

The historical can never be "had" as such. It is gone. It cannot be repeated and retested like a scientific experiment. It has no validity as mere analytical thought. It depends on untrained historical reporters who, technically speaking, were biased, and who, as believers, were ready and even craving to believe. *The pattern of Christ is in part the creation of confession.* None can go beyond this fact with regard to his historicity. Even so, a self-contained pattern in the teaching and life of Christ as Agape exists as a historic deposit, however little it can be demonstrated as a scientific measure or experiment. It is there for eyes to see, eyes cleansed of self-seeking by faith and hearts rid of mere search for security. It is there as a historic fact and as an objective pattern, but as a historic fact that must be subjectively entertained, grasped, "had," and understood. Once seen, the vision commands, like a third dimension once seen in a picture puzzle. Not seen, it still is there, but those who have not yet seen obviously cannot either see it or admit it. It is objective, but dependent for being seen on a special subjective insight.

Then, again, the objective Event-pattern of Christ as Agape is the ultimate context of Meaning only for a faith-judgment. Thus here too the subjective response is involved. None can prove the ultimate. Short of being God, we cannot prove God. There is no presuppositionless thinking. We all have an ultimate presupposition, organize experience in some total pattern beyond power of proof, and therefore live by faith. This is the irreducible truth of existential thinking. Rational, objective metaphysics assumes a static reality.

Thomism and Kantianism are both impotent at this point: Thomism because it has a metaphysics which Kant rightly demolished; Kantianism because it assumed for its categories a finished, static creation and never glimpsed the truth that metaphysics must now operate with a basically different key, in a keyhole not of being but of becoming. This critical category of becoming is no mere matter of dynamic change, but a matter of metaphysically authentic accumulative creation. Metaphysics must become post-Kantian, not defensively but to do justice to the facts of a whole new understanding of the world.

Existentialism, of course, no longer operates in a metaphysical framework. But neither has existentialism seen the truth of *real* becoming on account of which metaphysics becomes possible only by becoming religious. Metaphysics as *Weltanschauung* involves inescapably a faith-judgment at its basis. Metaphysics must now operate within the reality of creation as the ongoing process of novelty, and only the most high in process can be the best pointer to ultimate truth—a pointer not merely rational but also confessional.[28] The day of the classical kind of objective, rational metaphysics is done. The past cannot explain the present, and the mere description of the present, even hierarchically, leaves us flat, without ground for our having become, our present being, or our future becoming. Existentialism in the service of reason and within the context of an unavoidable faith, can give us the kind of metaphysics that is guilty

[28] See chaps. 3 and 4 of *Faith and Reason.*

neither of the *non sequiturs* of objective rational metaphysics nor of the meaninglessness of an individualistic existentialism. Heidegger's *existentiell* (*existenziell:* individualistic existentialism) can become *existential* (collectively responsible existentialism operating through a common human nature and situation) precisely through the understanding of becoming in the light of the selective actual with the capacity to become the co-ordinating Event of experience and existence.[29] We could not believe in Agape as the ultimate content for life and thought unless Agape truly satisfied both objectively and subjectively the requirements of a systematic method. Method itself demands that the objective real be dependent also upon the subjective response.

And finally, the subjective is more than the capacity for and the attainment of the intuitive grasp that affords objective insight and the click of conviction; and it is more than the situational requirement of a faith-judgment as to ultimate context of meaning; the subjective is also confessional in the sense that whereas sin prevents sight, faith provides a condition for seeing. Some cannot see the truth of Christ as ultimate within the true framework of God as Love, universally and unconditionally, either because they have never been so informed and come to see it, or because they have been looking at life and thought through limited or mixed perspectives. Such lack of seeing is a subjective failure due to objective reasons. Countless people, however, cannot see

[29] See chap. 4 of *Faith and Reason* for fuller explanation.

Christ as Agape because they will not.[30] They will not because they dare not or they dare not because they will not. Sin is both unfaithfulness through fear and fearfulness through rebellion. Actually Agape is such ultimate truth, requiring such wholeness of acceptance and such continual transformation of life to accord with it that mankind will try every device to dodge it. The best evasion is that which claims to be most Christian in terms of formal orthodoxy without the power and reality of the Gospel. By making such profession we can fool ourselves into thinking that we are confessing Christianity, and be most devoutly incensed if our profession is challenged. For this reason Agape still must be sent out as sheep among wolves, indeed, amidst very orthodox wolves!

God's truth, however, is its own best advocate and defense. What it needs is faithful proclamation. The Gospel is primarily not for saints, but for sinners to be made saints. Therefore even though the Gospel is high as heaven, it is yet come to earth in the fullness of time to bring us light and power unto salvation. Our task is as far as we can to set forth its full claim and promise. The result is safe and sound with God.

We have said in this chapter that we must determine

---

[30] How else could we be free and become real? How foreign to true theological understanding is, for instance, the following citation: "We may accordingly deny that modern approaches allow us to remain agnostically poised in regard to God: they force us to come down on the atheistic side. For if God is to satisfy religious claims and needs, he must be a being in every way inescapable" (J. N. Findlay, "Can God's Existence Be Disproved?" in Flew and MacIntyre, eds., *New Essays in Philosophical Theology,* p. 55).

with care our starting point. Individual and collective experience are necessary psychological and sociological starting points. We have to accept them for what they are. They cannot, however, be the starting point for theological method. We must start at the center, and neither our individual nor our collective experience is the center of Christology. The same is true of the Bible and of the great decisions concerning Christ taken by the major Ecumenical Councils. We have to take full cognizance of them, but they cannot constitute the criteria for right Christology. Only Christ himself as the truth, illuminating, judging and fulfilling all other truths, can be the adequate starting point methodologically for Christology.

The Christ who is Agape is the eternal Word by which all other words are interpreted and put in their proper place. When we as Christian believers dare to plumb Christianity's own radical depth—Christ as Agape—we shall fulfill Catholic Christianity in the freedom of truth and we shall continue the Reformation in the truth of freedom. A revolution in Christology and in religious thought will take place when Christianity dares to become radically Christian. Nothing short of such a revolution will discover and conserve the truth that both sets men free and leaves them secure in Christ.

II

VERY GOD, VERY MAN

I. THE HUMANITY OF JESUS

When I heard some people saying, "If I don't find it in the original documents, I don't believe it in the gospel," I answered them, "But it *is* written there." They retorted, "That's just the question." To my mind it is Jesus Christ who is the original documents. The inviolable archives are his cross and death and his resurrection and the faith that came by him. It is by these things and through your prayers that I want to be justified.[1]

THE Agape pattern of Jesus Christ, life and teacher, is the original document of our faith. He was not only as fully human as we, but more so, for in pristine power and in original fullness his humanity both shows what being human means, in its true and full sense, and demonstrates what is more than human in the genuinely human. Jesus is the human being who first conclusively fulfills the conditions of humanity, namely, to be organically united to God and fulfilled by the coinherence of God. Jesus lived love; God is love and has made men for love. As Adam symbolized the first poten-

---

[1] "Letter of Ignatius to the Philadelphians," in Richardson, ed., *Early Christian Fathers*, p. 110.

tial human being, the decisive step beyond animal creation, so Jesus, as Irenaeus saw, was the first true human being, in the sense of being fulfilled. His life was original as a new being of Agape. In a decisive sense the Son of Man is the Son of God. Only he among men who is genuinely Son of Man (*bar-nasha* or *ben-adam*) can be Son of God. The Son of Man becomes so only in relation to God as Son, the Word of God, the eternally pre-existent, personal Spirit who becomes enacted in man.

In Jesus, the truly human being, we meet God who is Agape, the creator, director, rescuer, and fulfiller of human lives and of human history. In Jesus we meet "the lowliness of man and the loftiness of Godhead." [2] While his "manhood was integral and essential and not merely instrumental," [3] "with no element lacking in his humanity that is necessary to man," [4] we meet in Jesus a new manhood, to the point where he became the Godman, God and man incommensurately but organically, and therefore victoriously, united. Thomas Torrance writes that "Jesus Christ is not only Word of God to man, but believer." [5] He represents both God and man.[6]

[2] "Tome of Leo," in Hardy, *Christology of the Late Fathers,* p. 364.

[3] Dr. F. W. Camfield quoted by Torrance in "The Atonement and the Oneness of the Church," *Scottish Journal of Theology,* Sept. 1954, p. 250.

[4] Hardy's summary statement of Origen's position in "Introduction" in *op. cit.,* p. 16.

[5] *Op. cit.,* p. 16.

[6] "Jesus Christ is not only God's freedom for man but man's freedom for God. He is not only God's electing of man, but man's choosing of God. The man who chooses, repents and trusts is Jesus" (Cochrane, *The Existentialists and God,* p. 45).

Very God, Very Man

The thesis of our theology is that we must start with the Incarnation—or with that personal event in history which most fully illuminates, judges and offers help for life while also indicating, through its very pointing of the cosmic process, the nature of ultimate reality. Such a thesis requires defining human nature itself in the light of its best example rather than reducing its truest specimen to less adequate examples. The best exceptional instance of man most generally exemplifies his potential nature. If with Jesus a new humanity came to be whereby the old human nature was transformed, we need to reclassify man. If such is the case, we must no longer define Jesus as human in terms of humanity in general or in terms less than himself. We now have a new definition of true manhood: Agape-man. If with Jesus we have a new class, a new level of life, or a new age of human history, a human nature that both fulfills and condemns as inadequate the old human nature, then we have no right to ascertain first what our human nature generally is in order to pare Jesus down accordingly to such a pattern.

Only, however, if Jesus shared ordinary human nature to begin with was he genuinely part of our history. The new humanity that was born from above in the life of Jesus constitutes a new start in history, in fact, a beginning which was also the end, for by it the true potential of human nature became actualized as the truly proper nature of man. But Jesus himself, being a true human being, did not begin with the transformed nature. He began where we all begin, with ordinary, actual human nature. He started with our full, common pedagogical nature, and ended with human nature perfected by its right relation to God—its free openness to Agape. In discussing the humanity of Jesus, however, we must start with his true humanity in the normative sense, his mature nature as the Godman and then relate his fulfilled humanity to ours, that is, to the kind he originally had, in the light of our common potential human nature in God. Hardy is right, it seems, in venturing to suggest that "the unity of God and man in Christ may be the commonly neglected side of Christology just now." [7] We start with our full perspective, in other words, and then analyze how this perspective originated and developed.

Rightly to define man, therefore, is to define him in the light of God, but much more, to define him as a victorious participant in the life of God. No man is fully man except a Godman—a person in whom human nature is organically fulfilled by its hypostatic union with God, for whom it is destined from the very beginning. To become fully human, therefore, is to be Godpossessed. It is to enter into a supernatural union with Godhead which is both the very nature of God when expressed in creation and, at the same time, our potential nature as intended in creation. This supernatural union of God and man is the crowning point of what is truly "natural" in the complete sense of that

[7] *Op. cit.*, p. 38.

term.[8] For this reason we do not speak of finality in Jesus, for growth is eternal, but rather with Baillie we commend the term "the determinative point" [9] as an accurate designation of Jesus' life. He is the conclusive or the fulfilling

---

[8] In this case the fullness of time came to be. We start with an actual fact of history, or with the fulfillment of meaning by Event. But the Event came to be by both the free and the conclusive response of man. God violated no human freedom by coming. Time became full by the confluence of God's presence and man's in the fulfilling Event of Agape. While man is thus kept free by asserting a realized rather than an actualized fullness of time, a fullness of time that could be known as a historic Event only after it came to be, God's freedom is also preserved by not being limited by any concrete revelation. We believe therefore that Barth has guarded God's freedom but not man's when he writes:

"There is no discoverable necessity compelling us to say of God that He had to do one thing and could not do something else.

"Augustine (*De Trin.* XIII 10) and Thomas Aquinas (*S. theo.* III, qu.1, art. 2c) rightly call attention to the fact that the freedom of God's almightiness must be respected here under all circumstances. 'To make any one of His revelations unconditionally necessary is to make Him dependent upon creatures' (F. Diekamp, *Kath. Dogm.,* Vol. 2, 1930, p. 187).

"But the statement in question [God had to become His own Mediator] can also be read off from the reality of revelation" (*Church Dogmatics I, 2,* p. 32).

In the long discussion that ensues Jesus Christ is cut off from man as a *"miraculous event"* (*Ibid.,* p. 63). God's revelation of Himself in Jesus Christ means that "God has time for us" and creates a special time in Jesus Christ, "the special direct act of God in the breaking in of new time into the midst of old" (*ibid.*). But man's freedom as real response is never allowed; therefore Jesus is not in fact part of human history in general, as a man among men, but a discontinuous event. No matter what Barth says about Christ's assuming our fallen nature and no matter how deep is his skepticism with regard to the historic Jesus, Barth never has a Christ with a genuine, full humanity. If God could choose the time and *create* it, without awaiting the fullness of time in terms of the free response of a human being, He would be an arbitrary God who does not meet or does not respect human freedom. We contend, rather, for an actual fullness of time when God's forceful initiative in coming declared His faithfulness by awaiting an actual response by Jesus. The response was in fact made within the total Godman relation, but was never subject to direct, immediate creation by God.

[9] *God Was in Christ,* p. 77.

point [10] of God's history with man, but never the concluding point either in Jesus or in other human beings. What Aulén called God's "Christ-deed" in the fullness of time is, as Brunner says, "a personal historical deed, a voluntary suffering and self-surrender," [11] that stands as the central focus of human history.

Yet man must also be seen in the light of his own history. To define man in terms of his ultimate relations is not enough; he must also be defined proximately. [12] The absolute and the relative must be seen together even while man is viewed from both perspectives, for although God and man are qualitatively distinct, eternally and radically, nevertheless they come together in the Godman and the Godmen. Out of two natures comes one genuine personality, neither simply God nor simply man, neither merely divine nor merely human, but Godman in such an integral manner that we may now no longer speak either of the divinely human or of the humanly divine. At the same time each remains true to its own nature without separation or confusion. Such is the nature of perfected humanity in its right relation to God.

Our task then is to ascertain the humanity of Jesus neither by picturing God in human form, a human being who really was God if seen at proper depth, nor by painting an ordinary human being apart from a revolutionary God-possession or

---

[10] "Other theologians have seen Jesus Christ as the consummator rather than the restorer of human nature" (J. L. M. Haire, "On Behalf of Chalcedon" in Parker, *op. cit.*, p. 95).

[11] *Eternal Hope,* p. 37.

[12] This is our objection to Dr. Thomas Torrance's urging us to define the humanity of Jesus only in the perfected sense of humanity.

the "enmanning" whereby God gave us His conclusive self-revelation and wrought our redemption. We need to see in Jesus a real human being, fulfilled by God to the point where God was the consummating co-Subject along with an accepting human subject, but both within a truly united and genuine personality. We need to see a man turned into the Godman to the point where our understanding both of God and of our history was changed radically and fulfillingly by his life. We shall so see him by means of a forthcoming analysis of the encounter of persons and the co-inherence of spirit in their dynamic interactions and distinctions.[13]

Human nature, at its origins, is characterized, at least, by a drive to selfhood, a desire for others and a need for God. Jesus had such a human nature. He shared our basic nature without qualification. Jesus had the same kind of self-drive, or *eros,* as ours by history and by creation. Part of this drive arose from bodily needs. He could be both tempted and wearied by them. Experiencing the precariousness of nature, he was tempted to throw himself down from the pinnacle of the Temple to prove his freedom from such

---

[13] Repeatedly we shall assert that such understanding is the central need of the Christian faith on its intellectual side. Barth, on the other hand, never tires of chanting the theme of the mystery of Christmas that *may not be investigated* (cf. *Church Dogmatics* I, 2, p. 126). He also calls in the Fathers to witness to this fact of a mystery by nature beyond man's understanding, even as is creation. But the Event has taken place and is now actually the intellectual key to human understanding, judgment and salvation. Woe unto us, therefore, if we hide behind reverence, worship and ontology, while the spiritual knowledge and power needed to match a world like ours is kept away from it by our failure to use the light that God has given us in Christ! A new creation took place; a new Being came to be; *but* we are now called both to enter and to understand this central relationship of God to man. On this point we differ decisively with Barth.

limitations, and finally a crude cross nailed down the fact of his subjection to physical precariousness and destruction. In contention with such limitations came the anxiety that he experienced in the wilderness and in Gethsemane. This self-centered *drive* of his life fed upon such anxiety, and made him wrestle "unto blood" with his freedom, crying "not my will, but thine be done."

Jesus also shared our desire for others. He chose disciples and called them friends. He cultivated an inner circle of followers. To what extent his ego-satisfactions in terms of others were stimulated and satisfied by being their leader we cannot know, but we do know that he actually entered into intimate social relationships. Jesus had friends in Bethany and knew, before that, the closeness of the family in which he was reared. On the other hand, he responded in sharp and hurt terms to the religious leaders who would not recognize his role and who kept others from accepting him. He knew the pain of being rejected in his own town. He complained over lack of response in the children of his generation. At the end of his life he asked the special support of the prayers of his intimate disciples for power to face his ordeal. Jesus' life clearly indicates this desire for others as well as the drive to self.[14]

Jesus also felt the need for God which expressed itself,

[14] We cannot dismiss these human responses as *merely* messianic and thus denude Jesus of his true and full humanity. Paul Minear has urged our considering these drives as messianic, which certainly they were, insofar as the Agape of God identified himself with the people; but unless we are to have an unreal human Jesus, we must accept the ordinary facts of his life for what they are.

as best we know, in his childhood at-homeness in the Temple, in his need to 'fulfil all righteousness" at his baptism, in his conquest of temptation, in his life of prayer, and finally, at the close, in both his struggle with God and the intimate acceptance of His will both in Gethsemane and on the Cross.

We cannot, of course, enter into the self-consciousness of Jesus.[15] We have a good deal of material that bears upon this question in form of reports, sayings, parables and stories, but we cannot now ascertain what Jesus himself felt. It is fair, however, to say that from what we do know, we can see that he had our full human nature with regard to its self-drive, its desire for others and its need for God. Such a nature he had in common with us. Yet as we look at his life we are amazed that its essential characteristic was a life of victory. This victory, moreover, was no mere report of an inner conquest of temptation, but an overt power in actual history to triumph over circumstance of rejection and defeat and to enable us to reorient our understanding of God and our own life. In the life of Jesus we encounter struggle and tensions of the most virile kind; we see even more, however, a power to face these struggles and to use these tensions as basic helps to the world.

With regard to his self-drive, the Godman never put himself in the place of God. If "sin is the act of finite freedom

---

[15] I am not attempting to depict "pure history" apart from presuppositions. Rather, I try to see facts in the light of my theologically and methodologically chosen perspective, Jesus as fully God and fully man. Years ago I read many books on the self-consciousness of Jesus, but never was persuaded by any of them.

to declare itself as unconditioned," [16] Jesus declared genuinely that "no one is good but God," and affirmed that the "Son of himself can do nothing." His victories in temptations reveal how he actually refused special status for himself. Even when he may have insisted that no one can come to God except through him, he identified his life with the shepherd who lays down his life for his sheep or with the Son who is killed in his father's service. He may thus have used himself as the sign and seal of love without which no one can know God. [17] With regard to others Jesus accepted both himself as leader and them as followers on the basis of understanding and co-operation. His was the freedom-giving love which required of his friends to face the cross and to take it up *with him for the world*. He neither sheltered his friends falsely nor used them to protect himself. His was a concern that forgave even those who crucified him, that cared for the disciples to the end, begging that they be spared, and that tended his mother's need while he himself hung pained on the cross. He knew family life, yet from the time of his temple visit at twelve years of age, he lived comparatively free of the family, it seems, in his

[16] Singh, *Preface to Personality,* p. 76. Cf. also Tillich's central use of this fact in his Christology.

[17] The reason I use "may" is that I hold the Synoptic Gospels and at least the primitive strands of the Acts of the Apostles to be more authentic, historical data than either the Gospel of John or Pauline material, in spite of the earlier date now attributed to John, and the very early dates of Paul's letters. All New Testament material outside the Synoptic Gospels and the primitive strands of the Acts of the Apostles are obviously too interpretative in nature to be used forthwith as historical material. This is especially true of the Letter to the Hebrews. This fact should be kept in mind throughout the rest of the book.

concern for his Father's business. Jesus' life throughout was characterized by identification with his people and with God's people.

Jesus' attitude to his mother may have appeared cruel and irresponsible when, anxious for his mental health, she came to fetch him, for he dismissed her as of no more importance to him than any other servant of God. Yet, may not this very rejection have shown his mission to transcend family limits? It may have caused him pain to say what seems hardhearted and unnecessary. He also appears to have been hemmed in by national prejudice in affirming that his mission was limited to the lost children of Israel, but he did accept the larger community as represented by the Syrophoenician woman even if growth in inclusion did cause him pain. We may think that he was vitriolic to the Pharisees and that he failed to understand their motivation, but if this firebrand was the historic person rather than the creation of the feelings of the persecuted disciples after his death, was he not mainly motivated by passion for genuineness and against religious self-righteousness? [18] Cannot the anger of Jesus in Mark 3:5, for instance, be the mark of signal concern? Were not these very passions the power which broke the old mold of religious piety and ushered in the inclusive love for all mankind within the love of God? Jesus is described

---

[18] I am aware of the understandably bitter feelings of Jewish interpreters of the New Testament at this point. It is very difficult for me to believe that Jesus' denunciation of the Pharisees is the authentic report *in detail*. At the same time, no one can say that they are not. Nor must I change their import. They stand, however, as a problem within the major conclusive context of Jesus' living and teaching Agape.

in the Letter to the Hebrews (5:7-9) as fearing death, while the Johannine writer tells us "there is no fear in love" (I John 4:18); but actually was it not his fathomless love of God and his concrete love for man in the main crises of his life that earned him the cross and gave him the power to face it and to bear it? Whatever be the struggle, he started within a nature like ours and he ended with a victory real enough and of sufficient depth to change the era of the world.

Before we undertake any more detailed analysis of the meaning and nature of Jesus' humanity, the fact ought to be clear that, as far as we know the records and as far as these records are backed by historic results, Jesus did share our full human nature, but in such a fulfilling manner as to lead us to say that he represents a new creation in history.[19] The old human nature was there genuinely, but somehow it became freed from its ordinary drags to the degree where victory was really won over man's basic tempta-

[19] This affirmation is true whether we think we can get back to an authentic pattern of the historic Jesus in terms of life, teachings, death and resurrection, or whether we start with the *kerygma* concerning Christ as proclaimed in the New Testament. I cannot see that Kähler solved the historical problem by insisting that the nature of the New Testament is to urge us to believe in Jesus Christ and that therefore we should deal with its message. The *kerygma* itself should certainly take cognizance of the actual Christ depicted by the New Testament, not go on to a glorified theological figure; for the real glory of the New Testament is the pattern of the power of Agape that wins the victory in the midst of the full humanity. Critical history may be limited by numerous details, but it can legitimately and must critically go at least that far in presenting the historic basis of the faith. I do not like the word myth, but if G. V. Jones is positively understood, I can agree that Jesus' life is a "metaphysical myth," at least that it is a historic event not subject to critical assessment in the strict sense, but having transcendent meaning, and, I believe, reality (*op. cit.*).

tions. The human nature of Jesus participated in the life of God with such transforming power that his life became not only the hope for a new history but also the help to attain it. The Son of Man acquired such a humanity by accepting the Son of God. Yet even before such acceptance was possible, God the Son had Himself come to Jesus and by His presence and calling had made possible the Son of Man who became "the pioneer and perfecter of our faith" (Heb. 12:2). *The precedence and priority always lie with God, even in the case of human nature, but they lie always in a faithful relation to human response. The Son of God and the Son of Man thus keep coming together from the beginning of creation but actually become fulfilled together at one consummating point in human history!*

Humanity became *itself* in a conclusive sense in Jesus. We have barely indicated in Jesus a kind of humanity that, although pressured by ordinary drives, is under the direction of higher *motivation*. Humanity became full in Jesus as the representative Head of a new humanity. Jesus enmanned not only a new single man, but a new man generically, potentially and representatively.[20] He was the new Israel.

[20] It is both a sad and a significant fact that Barth can write: "We have seen earlier that what the eternal Word made His own, giving it thereby His own existence, was not a man, but man's nature, man's being, and so not a second existence, but a second possibility of existence, to wit, that of a man" (*op. cit.*, p. 163). Instead of the Word fulfilling man organically, according to God's nature and man's, the true humanity of Jesus, specifically as *a* man, the Word so to speak creates manhood for the Christ specially for Him. Thus Jesus is not a man in our sense, but a man only as a distinct, individual being in history who experienced the Word. Thus Barth can write, for instance: "It is in virtue of the eternal Word that Jesus Christ exists as a man of flesh and blood in our sphere, as a man like us, as an historical

Having set forth Jesus as our new humanity, we shall now suggest how human nature was prepared for its new fullness. After that we shall show something of human nature as it is in the fullness of time, when the pressures of the old man are dissolved by the power of the new motivation.

Whatever be the exact form of evolution, mankind has developed from below via some route of animal life; such is at least the case for the raw stuff of human nature. Above the creative swirl has hovered the Spirit, waiting to ignite man from above with the living flame of life, or to breathe the breath of life into the body formed from the dust of the ground, that is, from the evolutionary process as such. Man by nature consists of tamed drives. He is domesticated in nature by God. Man has a fierce drive to self: defensively, to secure and to protect life; and aggressively, to augment and to enrich it. The drive to self is seen in civilized life mostly in terms of the subconscious, especially when it is laid bare in pathological states, or in the crises of life and death. Although man is "socialized," this state is mostly a matter of concealing the real self behind social conventions

---

phenomenon" (*ibid.,* p. 165). Actually Barth stresses intensely the manhood of Christ, even while he is never able to discard the Grand Myth of God walking in a human body or in a human organism rather than coming integrally into an ordinary human being who was fully one of us. Christology will be magic and mockery until we take seriously the full Godhood and manhood of Jesus and begin to see all else in this real fact of history. Such an actual life becomes Dorothy Emmet's "co-ordinating analogy" (*The Nature of Metaphysical Thinking*) or my own "selective actual" (*Faith and Reason*). I use co-ordinating *Event* as directly explanatory rather than as analogy. Barth's words and direction start out well. His intention seems to be to know the full humanity of Jesus, but he does not carry it through.

and channeled behavior. Men learn to say and, for social purposes, to feel what is expected of them—they become domesticated by God in nature mostly through history. Men still have, nevertheless, however deep down it may lie, the will to power, to publicity and to protection from all harm to self. They therefore resent having to inhibit their drives. The temptation stories show plainly that Jesus shared these drives as actual inner powers that he had to combat.[21]

Domesticated man, however, learns to live under the law. The law becomes the necessary factor for community where the drives have to be combatted. The outer part of law is sanctions; the inner part is duty. The keeping of the law is righteousness, and involves right relations. John the Baptist preached the law and baptized for the remission of sins. He ordered the penitent to do justly, to keep the law. Even Jesus felt the need to be thus baptized in order to fulfill all righteousness. He, too, shared the drives of men which make law necessary. When he encountered those who represented the reign of law, particularly of God's law, he wanted voluntarily to conform. In this identification with the order of righteousness, he acknowledged the presence of God. Going out "full of the Holy Spirit" (Luke 4:1), however,

---

[21] A spiritualistic pride conceives of sin as unrelated to man's physical drives, as unrelated to his natural and historical past; but sin is of the whole man, the concrete man, the man of flesh and bone (Unamuno) and not only of the spirit. Sin is basically faithlessness resulting in rebellion against God, perversion of self, and selfishness toward others. But sin is never apart from the actual occasions of the whole man in his concrete, natural and social environment. (See *The Christian Faith,* chap. 6)

he was tempted not to be under law, but rather to be above it, and to impose the law on others by means of power.[22]

There are two kinds of conflicts within: suppression and repression. Suppression is a matter of conscious conflict; repression, of unconscious conflict. Jesus seems to have known both kinds. The temptations, on the one hand, are overt experiences. On the other hand, the heat with which Jesus rejects the Syrophoenecian woman in her request that her daughter be healed—contending that he was sent only to the lost children of Israel—indicates the subconscious incubation of the larger vision and the deeper hurt in the acceptance of his mission to men as men, a vision and a mission which later had to be saved once more by Paul at the Council of Jerusalem and in his own missionary activity. There is therefore no reason to suppose that Jesus had no subconscious in the ordinary sense of drives and of repressions.[23] When Jesus looked around with anger (Mark 3:5), such anger may not merely have been righteous concern, which seldom in its purity expresses itself in anger, but may also have been the result of mixed motives. He was grieved at the hardness of their heart; but all the same his own breaking of the Sabbath in the interest of healing very

[22] To interpret the temptations as merely messianic is to rob them of their sharp actuality and of their personal character. This statement, however, in no way reduces these experiences to the realm of the merely personal.

[23] This fact is one of my objections to the explanation of the sinlessness of Jesus by W. R. Matthews (*The Problem of Christ in the Twentieth Century*). He declares that lacking our common kind of subconscious mind, Jesus could know mankind's original sin in his consciousness without yielding to it.

likely did not come about without some inner strife, part of which probably went below conscious conflict. Our actual evidence, to be sure, is slight and therefore bears little weight, but of what we have there is enough to suggest that the behavior of Jesus *was genuinely human in terms of the ordinary tensions which men must bear, both from without and from within.*

Men, moreover, are tempted to sin not only because others have sinned before them, setting them an example and providing for them a lure, and because they seem to be really caught in a sinful order, but also because each man as an individual has the desire to lord it over others; or because anxiety in the face of death leads to the fear that is the letting go of faith. No one, of course, can sin for anyone else; therefore "original" sin cannot be inherited *as sin,* but only as the occasion for sin or as the drive toward sin from within a common human nature. Such "original" sin, as we have seen, is both of a self-drive and of a social kind. Jesus knew the drive to power over others, as exhibited in his temptations; he knew also the will to save the self from death in the struggle of Gethsemane and he had enough self-objectification to recognize this drive as the voice of self overagainst the will of God. He also learned obedience to law—not only its cost!—by his suffering, knowing personally the conflict of duty and crying from fear day and night to him who could save him from death (Heb. 5:7). If we may use such long-distance reporting as the Letter to the Hebrews,[24] he was well acquainted with the drive of self to escape the human predicament.

We should therefore acknowledge, from the evidence we do have, that Jesus shared our tendency to power and to self that are the occasions for sin. If original sin is defined as acquiescence in the sinful status quo, while being subject to "original" sin is defined as the occasion for sin, then Jesus did not share in the sin itself. Jesus also genuinely expressed the fear that is the absence of the full faith of love, the inner *acceptance of anxiety*. Otherwise there is no accounting for his temptations and his grievous struggles. Perfect love throws out fear and "whatsoever does not proceed from faith is sin" (Rom. 14:23). In the sense of sharing the origins and the burdens of moral struggles Jesus obviously was "made sin" (II Cor. 5:21). We shall see that such a realistic view of the nature of Jesus makes possible a genuine experience of Incarnation. Love cannot be imposed from without as a substance nor grown organically, like a plant; love must be received freely by a person who has tasted the struggles of self and who can become mature only by standing apart even from God.

With Jesus, nevertheless, there seems to be a radical shift in human nature in the sense that, as far as we can tell, these drives, however genuine, were made to serve the development of an authentic personal experience learning through decisions and growing in the face of temptations.

[24] No wonder that Windisch in his commentary on the epistle, *Der Hebräerbrief,* concludes that the doctrine of the sinlessness of Jesus was born out of a theological context!

The answer to the arrival of such a basically new human nature seems to be the presence of God in Jesus or the presence of Jesus with God. Jesus' life of prayer most fully indicates this togetherness, this symbiosis. There was a participation of God in the life of Jesus and of Jesus in the life of God that both held in control and used for real victory the genuine drives of "original" sins. The raw nature of man—often explained by traditionalistic theologians as due to "the fall" [25]—rumbled within, but these drives became the occasion for a new level of living, where the human self knew that it was fulfilled by the will and power of the divine self.

God became the co-subject of man; [26] thereby also enhancing man as subject. Only when man acts within God and within the will of God for him, does he find his true self and his own fulfillment. Therefore the self, in that God is its co-subject, finds the unity of a personality which is no longer torn by drives or driven by duty, but released for its true nature within the power of God. [27] The truly

[25] We know of no historic fall and therefore may not use "the fall" as a chronological-causal category. The drives are not merely or mostly physical, as the temptations in the wilderness attest. Again, I repeat, to define sin merely in terms of the spirit of man and not in terms of the whole, actual man is to be guilty either of partial or prideful thinking. Man sins as a creature, in relation to a total self that includes the physical, and not as a god or a pure spirit.

[26] I shall show later how co-inherence in the category of Spirit makes for an integrated rather than a split or a possessed personality.

[27] The whole way through I assume the two-nature theory. This makes sense to me as nothing else does. In fact it is the light for all theological thinking at its center. For me, therefore, G. C. Berkouwer's starting point of his book, *The Person of Christ*, is not so vivid as it perhaps should be: "Preoccupation with the many problems which, in the course of history, have

natural or "real" self is thus the self where God is the most fully co-subject of human experience. Yet freedom or control within God does not preclude a continuing struggle, for the drives of self and of duty remain in order to be the occasion for ever fuller and deeper growth in God and in self-reality. The drives of self, when fulfilled by being directed aright by the Spirit and motivated effectively by Him, *make the self social in God and social with men, even while making the self an ever more real and growing person.*

Thus, Jesus' victories in the wilderness did not make unnecessary his struggle in Gethsemane. The full, final victory of man over all drives comes only when the Spirit has taught him the glorious liberty and fulfillment within the will of God so deeply and so long that temptation cannot occur. Temptation finds no place of appeal in the finally mature person. Full deliverance from conflict is not even then assured because of outer conflicts that invade and tend to disrupt the inner maturity, but now these conflicts occur no longer as temptations, but as objects for concern and for

---

arisen around the person of Jesus Christ is bound to reveal the undeniable fact that one can speak without exaggeration of a far-reaching crisis in the dual-nature doctrine. The old confession of the church, that Jesus Christ was truly God and truly man, has increasingly become the object of radical criticism" (p. 21). Indeed, my whole approach is one of wonder that the Christian Church has never dared to make the two-nature understanding of Christ central not only to theological explanation but to metaphysics as well. (Cf. *Faith and Reason* and *Christian Understanding of God* as books implicitly or explicitly built on this cornerstone.) Schleiermacher's charge in his *Der Christliche Glaube* that the two natures are so dissimilar or incommensurate that they cannot coexist can be made only because there is no basic Christian metaphysics in his thinking. Our understanding of all basic problems of life, history and creation, however, center in their actual relation to God.

helping. Full inner maturation and outer solution of conflicts, however, may never come in this life, and therefore
the Resurrection of Jesus might well stand for the symbol
of maturation and solution. In this life Jesus had the victory
which controls, but does not eliminate, temptations. The
full union of God with man, in any case, requires a genuine
struggle and long growth. Apart from such growth through
temptation and struggle, through overagainstness and alienation, there is no human nature expressive of God's general
preparation in experience through history for the coming
of the new creation, the new human nature in Christ and in
the new community in the Spirit.

Thus we have shown that Jesus both had full human
nature and historic development, as a growing person, and
also attained full human nature, in the normative sense of
the fulfillment of man within the right relation to God
or within His dominantly motivating Presence. Grensted
speaks of this fact when he writes: "To the psychologist
they speak plainly enough of a life in which there is, from
the Baptism, a full and complete turning to God, and yet
in which there is progressive unification." [28] The humanity
of Jesus in the sense both of growth and of fulfillment
is a precondition for the relevance of his life for ours
and for the assurance we may truly have of the victory of
Agape in life as a historic power, and in eternity. In the
deepest sense we can say with regard to sin, law and death,
as does Richard Baxter, "Christ leads me through no darker

[28] *The Person of Christ,* p. 279.

93

rooms than He went through before," and with Sir Edwyn
Hoskyns that "the whole New Testament rings with a sense
of freedom from sin." [29] The humanity of Jesus, as we shall
see, is the key both to God's assuming our sin, and what is
more, to His conquest of it. A full humanity receives the
fullness of God, thus radically fulfilling the meaning of
both life and history. God is Love; and our being within
the Love of God is the only final, fulfilling answer to the
nature and problems of humanity.

II. ANAKEPHALAIOOSIS AND ENHYPOSTASIA

If we view the humanity of Jesus from both the perspective of victory and the perspective of its preparation through
all our ordinary drives, we arrive at an understanding in
which Jesus is both the summit and the summary of human
nature. We see Jesus as the divine discontinuity transforming
the human continuity within a genuine personality that is
both God and man. Jesus is God-man and Godman. God-man
means that he came to be Godman through a real process
of coming together in which both God and man participated,
although, of course, God had incomparably the initiative
and the consummating power. God-man, in other words,
stands for the reality of both the divine and human natures
with all their distinctive capacities, while Godman expresses
the eventual unity of the historic personality of Jesus. The
Christ was the Godman. In Jesus there eventuated complete
unity of personality without fusion of natures. How did

[29] *The Riddle of the New Testament*, p. 219.

such a personality come to be and what is involved in it? Our first consideration will be how Jesus became the God-man, or how "the Word became flesh." This topic we shall discuss under Irenaeus' doctrine of *anakephalaioosis*. What is involved in such a Godman we shall then discuss under the headings of *anhypostasia* and *enhypostasia*. *Anakephalaioosis* is the doctrine that Jesus recapitulated the history of the race through the whole course of his obedience (Irenaeus). *Anhypostasia* claims with Cyril of Alexandria and especially with Leontius of Byzantium [30] that Jesus had no human nature independent of the hypostatic union, or of his Godward side; while *enhypostasia* affirms that within the hypostatic union Jesus had a genuine human nature.

The way Irenaeus puts his doctrine of *anakephalaioosis* (recapitulation) is that Jesus "would not have had real flesh and blood, by which he paid the price, unless he had indeed recapitulated in himself the ancient making of Adam." [31] In our day we believe no longer in Adam as an instantaneous creation of man, but rather in man's long evolving through a process of natural and human history under the creative power of God, sparked by his Spirit. But whether we put the creation of man in Irenaeus' terms or in those of our own day, the point in each instance is the same: the Son of God became man not by some special creation of human-ity, but rather precisely by his partaking of the original making of man. The reason for the assertion is also the

[30] Migne, *Greek Patrologia*, Vol. 86.
[31] "Against Heresies," in Richardson, *op. cit.*, p. 386.

same, namely, that the eternal Word might enter genuinely into our humanity and pay the price of our salvation from within our actual nature and situation. Gregory Nazianzus once wrote to the same effect: "For that which he has not assumed he has not healed; but that which is united to his Godhead is also saved. If only half Adam fell, then that which Christ assumes and saves may be half also." [32] Hardy in introducing the *Christology of the Late Fathers* calls this statement "Gregory's keynote." [33] Prestige, commenting on this statement, writes similarly that "there can be no true salvation of human beings from within, through the regeneration of their own nature, when the Savior Himself has no genuine human experience." [34] Jesus cannot be less, only more, human than we. As Irenaeus phrased it, Adam was the first potential man while Jesus was the first actual human being. He became so by recapitulating in himself the actual making of man from the beginning; thus Jesus was the summary as well as the summit of human nature.

What can we mean today by Jesus' recapitulating human nature? We need, first of all, to accept the simple fact that Jesus was a human being. He was not merely man in some impersonal sense; he was *a* man. As such he inherited his human nature in the same manner as anyone else. His life went back to the very beginning of life's coming to be on earth. His biological tissue, with its strains and stresses, went back to before the Ice Age. His mental make-up and

[32] "Letters on the Apollinarian Controversy," in Hardy, *op. cit*, p. 218.
[33] *Ibid.*, p. 31.
[34] *Fathers and Heretics*, p. 113.

mental environment came from human history as such, and from his specific history in Palestine as well. Before any child is born it repeats the history of the race in the womb, and after birth it repeats the history of its people as it is relevant to the child. In no way was Jesus different with regard to his humanity from any normally born child. Only by being fully and normally human could Jesus enter entirely and organically into our human predicament. As a matter of fact, as we have seen, our starting point is with the historical, not with the mythical nature of Jesus' life. The actual life of Jesus—with its birth, growth, mission, teachings, death and resurrection—lies as the bedrock basis of our view of God, for through this Person and event we most fully meet the nature of God, to light, to judge and to save us. There should be, therefore, no trace of suspicion of our manufacturing any mythical account for the purposes of Revelation. *Anakephalaioosis* should be the strongest antidote to docetism; recapitulation ought to insure the true and full humanity of Jesus.

D. M. Baillie, after years of careful work, asserted that "it is plain that we find in the New Testament both the very highest claims for the divine revelation in Jesus and the very frankest recognition that He was a man." [35] A critical historian must begin at this point. It is unnecessary to recite again evidence of the humanity of Jesus, such as his own sayings: "Why callest thou me good? None is good but God." "I can of myself do nothing, as I hear, I judge,"

[35] *Op. cit.,* p. 125.

and other instances of similar nature. Nor need we trace
the development of titles attributed to Jesus from *Quellen*
and *UrMark* to some such point as the Book of Revelation.
Even as late as the Pastoral Epistles it is stated that "there
is one God, and there is one mediator between God and
men, the man [*anthropos*] Jesus Christ" (I Tim. 2:5). All
such analytical studies of manuscripts, however, fall far
short of the original facts because all manuscripts, by the
very nature of historic accumulation in the transmission of
materials, contain the splendid but historically specious de-
velopments of devotion and piety. While *theologically* we
must begin with the nature and work of God in the Incarnation, since priority belongs necessarily to the ultimate category, *historically* we must begin with the genuine, natural
humanity of Jesus. However much historic interpretation
may elucidate eternal realities symbolized by history and
however much man must live by history as though it were
eternity, solid scholarship must aim at the facts which later
become the occasion for the work of piety and devotion.

A real doctrine of *anakephalaioosis* thus precludes *anhypostasia* (no human nature apart from the hypostatic union)
insofar as the latter doctrine contends for a human nature
which was specially created or came into being at the time
of the hypostatic union. If the hypostatic union is defined
as "very God and very man" in organic fulfillment within a
genuine human personality, such hypostatic union in order
to contain "very man" presupposes full preparation of human
nature in history on the part of both God and man for

the conclusive consummation. If God entered man in such a manner that he did not share the full history of mankind, there was no real Incarnation; there was only God in a human body, a theophany. Jesus would have been in this case different from us as human beings. Both the form of God and the form of man must involve the full nature of God and the full nature of man. A marked abuse of *anhypostasia* in history has, in fact, been to introduce the sub-Christian idea of an impersonal humanity of Jesus. There is no impersonal humanity that is "very man"! Such a notion is just as inadequate, on the other side, as an impersonal Word entering into the union, becoming personal in Jesus.

The theological mischief made possible by certain interpretations of the biological doctrine of the Virgin Birth begins to become apparent at this point. The real danger is the abuse of this doctrine, to separate Jesus from his full humanity and ours.[36] Historically the evidence for such an event is weak, particularly because of its absence both in the original Gospel, Mark, and in the earliest of all Christian records, the letters of Paul. Paul, by nature, drove home with burning zeal all that he believed to be intrinsic to the Gospel. The belief in the Virgin Birth, besides, is no part of the primitive teaching of the Apostles as recorded in the Acts of the Apostles. When we add to these facts its absence in the

---

[36] Cf. G. V. Jones, *Christology and Myth in the New Testament,* p. 183: "The Christological consequences of the [birth] narratives, however, must be faced: that it represents Jesus not only as involved 'organically' in humanity, but also as separated from the human series by a radical discontinuity with it."

Johannine literature and, indeed, in all other New Testament writings than in the two birth stories in Matthew and Luke, the case for the Virgin Birth becomes tenuous. Even Matthew and Luke make no use of this highly significant claim in their later discussions of Jesus' relation to his parents. After a careful study of the problems, moreover, connected with these two birth stories themselves, the critical historian will very likely cast his lot with fact rather than with personal piety or with institutional pressures.[37] The most forceful argument against the inclusion of the Virgin Birth in the Gospel, however, is not historical but theological. The abuse indicated above seems to be one basic reason for its assertion. The doctrine of the Virgin Birth is too often used, at least psychologically, to preclude a full doctrine of Incarnation. Jesus in such a case is no longer fully one of us. He is discontinuous with us from the start.

The doctrine of the Virgin Birth, in its natural sense, may exclude a full doctrine of the Incarnation because God's coming into history involved the full genuine union of God and man. The Virgin Birth also debars the full humanity of Jesus if the doctrine is used to insure Jesus from the power of sin because he came as God ready-made, so to speak. Love must be learned by human beings and accepted through

[37] The doctrine of the Virgin Birth, however, must have appeared early in Christian history, very likely within the first few decades. Historically, as far as manuscripts go, both the absence and the presence of the claim go far back to Christian beginnings, but the absence from the earliest manuscripts is decisive. Therefore we should put the case of heresy as to the Virgin Birth in the opposite way from Monsignor Duchesne when he writes: "*L'hérésie, nous l'avons vu, est contemporaine de l'Evangile.*" (*Histoire Ancienne de L'Eglise,* I, p. 153.)

struggle and alienation, at least as a free, critical decision of maturation, and not imposed or implanted as a substance. Any theology which insists that God was fully present from birth may in upholding one truth, the primacy of God's coming throughout the whole event of Incarnation, deny the other, the need for real growth in grace and wisdom. For this reason insistence on the Virgin Birth as preclusive of true freedom is emotionally of critical importance for all docetists and for all who want to escape the full judgment on man as men and the full promises to him that are involved in the fact of the Incarnation. Let us examine this truth.

While the purpose and presence of God in man and in human history are fulfilled by the final fellowship of the sons of God, the nature and destiny of man also come to their fruition by man's mature participation in the presence and purpose of God. Mature participation, however, comes only after moral struggle, alienation from God and men, and the consequent willing and loving acceptance of God and of all men. A main purpose of creation is that men not only might be free to sin but actually that they might live estranged from God, at least in the sense that God's will might not be the easy or "natural" choice for man. *Without such freedom, alienation and understanding acceptance there is no true human nature* in the preparatory sense.

The Virgin Birth, however, may be interpreted to endow Jesus, *before or at birth,* with the full nature of God, even as the center of his ego, in such a way that he could not sin.

Therefore, on such a presupposition Jesus was never and could never be free to sin. God cannot sin, of course, because God cannot deny Himself. If God, then, came into Jesus as a determinative substance before Jesus had any real human history, then God merely took on human flesh without human form, or a human organism without human nature. Then God never became man in the sense of His being organically united to man and fulfilling him, but instead, God walked disguised in a human body, much as an actor appears in a strange guise.[38] Thus *anhypostasia* in relation to the Virgin Birth easily becomes a denial of the Incarnation. God, in such a case, never assumed our full human predicament nor did He solve it from within, but He merely put aside, for the time being, certain powers as God that He might appear human; and sampled, so to speak, our earthly conditions.

What was not assumed, however, was not healed! The

---

[38] The Letter to the Hebrews, if the phrase "yet without sinning" (4:15) is the addition of a pious but not wise theological editor, has a remarkable passage moving Jesus, the High Priest, from the order of Aaron to the order of Melchizedek. The Aaronic high priest offers up sacrifices both for himself and for his people. He does not presume to take such responsibility upon himself but is, rather, called by God to do it. Even so Jesus, not exalting himself, was called of God, even "begotten of God," but made a high priest of the order of Melchizedek only after he had been made perfect (Heb. 5:1-10). Having been made thus perfect and begotten of God on that day, he could be fittingly "blameless, unstained, separated from sinners" (Heb. 7:26). Now need he no longer offer up daily sacrifices because once and for all he had offered himself up for his own sin and for that of the people (Heb. 7:27). This high priest, now "perfect forever" (Heb. 7:28), yet has tasted and assumed the whole experience and burden of our guilt and can always understand our situation. Through such a victorious high priest we now draw near with confidence to the throne of grace. He has enacted a new covenant based on better promises!

whole purpose of the Incarnation is in such a case forfeited; instead of having God organically joined to man according to His eternal purpose, co-conquering with man and in man, we now have a mechanical and an external understanding of the life of Jesus, his death and his resurrection. Jesus as man, then, was not even tempted, while as God he conquered apart from man (contrary to the assertion of Gregory Nazianzus) for, being determinatively God from the beginning, his temptations were other than those of human beings and his victory was a foregone conclusion. In such a case Jesus raised himself as God from the grave rather than having been raised by God. Nor is Jesus then really our brother, the firstborn among many brethren who could meaningfully say "my God and your God" (John 20:19).

Anhypostasia, whatever the complete intent may have been that underlay its original use, actually operates to cut Jesus off from human nature. To do so is to destroy the meaning of the Incarnation, namely, that God knew our human nature from within. Even as at Nicaea the Church insisted that Jesus was consubstantial with God, and as at Constantinople, that he was consubstantial with man, even so we must now continue this insistence by rejecting the doctrine of *anhypostasia* as connected with the Virgin Birth. The full union was *of* God not *like* God and *of* man not *like* man. If the nature of God in his fullness was only *given* in birth, not actualized but held passive, quiescent, recessive, so that Jesus actually grew not only in body and in mind but also in moral insight and in decisions, learning obedience through what he suffered and thus becoming mature as "the pioneer and perfecter of our faith," then there is little theological reason for the biological doctrine of the Virgin Birth. If the Virgin Birth in any way endows Jesus with a predetermined sinlessness or, even more, with some initial presence of God which sets him off essentially from normal human beings, then the Son of God never took on our human nature. Then we have, in fact, no real doctrine of the Incarnation as the full union of God's and man's nature.

Anhypostasia, however, need not stand for a separation of Jesus from man, in the sense that he assumed some impersonal or general human nature without full participation in our ordinary human nature, including our moral struggle and genuine moral growth; for *anhypostasia* can stand for the reality of a new human nature wrought in Jesus by means of his effective hypostatic union with God. For such a transformation to take place organically, Incarnation must be conceived of as an *event in history,* not as a descent on humanity from outside without need for historic time and historic decision. *Anhypostasia* then signifies Christ as the new creature through whom we can become new creatures in Christ. *Anhypostasia* then declares that human nature in the hypostatic union is special, other than, more than and uniquely different from our ordinary nature. The Christ was born in the fullness of time, and the moment of conclusive union is whenever there was a full fruition, *organically,* of the presence and purpose of God and the nature and destiny of man.

The doctrine of the Virgin Birth, then, feels for the fact that when the Incarnation takes place not only can God come only from God, but there is even involved in this birth—primarily neither "of blood nor of the will of the flesh nor of the will of man, but of God" (John 1:13)—actually and stubbornly a new kind of human nature, a discontinuous dimension imposed on the level of human nature as it was before this new creation in Jesus, a new arriving that fulfills previous continuity. The Virgin Birth then can be made to stand for the miracle of the conception of the Son of God in human history on the side both of God and of man. At its heart the traditional doctrine makes the right assertions, but places the miracle at the wrong time and all too often makes the assertion for the wrong reasons. Such a distortion of doctrine can be due partially to our willingness as men to escape the judgment of the true light upon us and the call to our own "Virgin Birth." The Early Church still had such a right conception when the early Christians wrote on the baptistery of the Lateran Church in Rome: "In virgin birth the Church conceives her children in the Spirit of God and gives birth to them in water." [39] More and more the doctrine has actually been used to contend for the denial of the Incarnation, to the effect that Jesus could not sin because he was God and that even on his human side he was inimitably different from us, not only as our forerunner, but as the only one thus born.

[39] Michael Schmaus, *Katolische Dogmatik,* IV, I, p. 116. I owe this observation to Professor Thomas Torrance.

The doctrine of *anhypostasia,* however, need not be used to deny *anakephalaioosis.* It can stand, instead, for the important truth that in the coming to be of the hypostatic union there was no human nature apart from the intimate and conclusive activity of God. Such a claim does not have to involve the assumption of a nature created anew for Jesus, free from original sin and from the stained history of man, but can stand, rather, for the fact that human nature is never apart from God at any stage, and least of all at its consummation. Any definition of man apart from God is always incorrect. Through the whole process of human history God has taken the supreme initiative and does so in the case of every life. *Anakephalaioosis* and *anhypostasia* therefore require each other. Just as no life is born or develops apart from a human history which it recapitulates, so no human being is ever born or develops apart from God. In the second place, however, and of critical importance, *anhypostasia* stands for the fact that when the Agape-centered life of man became mature in Jesus, this nature was a new creation, explainable only in terms of God. In Jesus occurred a special event in history; in him was born a new human nature; in him came the fullness of time. Thus viewed the doctrine of *anhypostasia* fulfills the very meaning of *anakephalaioosis*—at least insofar as human nature and human history are seen from within the perspective of the eternal purpose of God in Christ Jesus.

Enhypostasia, moreover, or an independent human nature within the hypostatic union, is a necessary doctrine both before and after the union. The human nature of Jesus was independent of the full constraint of Godhood until Jesus learned through moral conflict, and thus having been made perfect became the author of our salvation. The Son of God was not thrust into a human body nor thrust on human nature. God is Love and He does not therefore give Himself to us like a gift in a package. There has to be human response to God's love if it is to be given and received. Only through love can God send His Son. There was therefore preparation for his coming in the people of Israel, in the family into which Jesus was born, particularly in the life of Mary his mother, and in the experience of Jesus himself. The conclusive initiative was God's, both from the beginning and throughout the whole process. Especially He poured himself with climactic fullness into the life of Jesus, both calling him and enabling him for the most crucial task in human history, to become the Godman, not that either God or he ever originated the eternal Son for God as Son is as eternal as God Himself, being of God, from God and God; nevertheless, the *Godman* became *in* history and *by* history as well as *in* eternity and *by* eternity. The eternal Word *became flesh* in history.

Enhypostasia as a doctrine consequently demands that we reject outright Cyril's contention that, as Prestige puts the case, the self of God the Son, "appropriately limited and conditioned," became "the personal subject of the manhood of Christ." [40] Today men like Brunner and Micklem have

40 Prestige, *op. cit.,* p. 162.

taken somewhat the same line.[41] Such a viewpoint is definitely akin to that of Apollinaris; it sells Jesus' humanity short. The personality of Jesus was an organic, though incommensurate, union of God and man; the ego was therefore neither human nor divine, separately or together, but a new creature fulfilling both, where part remains uncreate for ever, without beginning and end, while the other remains created, becoming eternal only within the hypostatic union. We cite Gregory Nazianzus again: "What he was he continued to be; what he was not he took to himself . . . having converse with flesh by means of mind." [42] Although the following statement is not altogether correct, nevertheless it is generally so, and bears down hard on the central fact: "While his inferior [nature], the humanity, became God, because it was united to God, and became one [person] because the higher nature prevailed . . . in order that I too might be made God so far as He is made man." [43] The higher nature prevailed, with the lower nature struggling, but becoming willing, until there was a full response of one integrated personality who conclusively enacted the Agape life of God, by participating in the life of God at the center of his personality, while also having and ever retaining his human nature. In Jesus this union became sufficiently genuine for God, through him, to open the heaven

[41] Cf. Brunner, *The Mediator,* and Micklem, *Ultimate Questions.*
[42] *Theological Orations,* III, p. 19.
[43] *Ibid.*

for us, to make a way of grace from eternity to the ends of created time, and thereby to change the whole stream of human history.

Enhypostasia, then, should stand for the genuineness of the human nature both in preparation for the fullness of time and in the fullness of time. The elder Gregory opposed any such view as the former of these: "If any assert that the manhood was formed and afterward was clothed with the Godhead, he too is to be condemned." [44] His stricture is right if human nature is thought of as independent of God so that a man became righteous through his own merit and was rewarded by God because of his good desert. Such a view is both adoptionist and Pelagian. The idea that man can be or become righteous apart from God is vicious deism and moralism. The idea that God should become united to man because of, or in proportion to, his independent righteousness denies the whole need for grace as central to God's purpose with history and the whole need for man's alienation, which alone makes any sense out of historic existence as pedagogically necessary. If, however, Gregory's denial is taken to be due to some belief in *anhypostasia,* in the sense of a special human nature for Jesus that was peculiarly united to Godhood in such a manner that he never shared our desperate plight as human beings, not only because of death and finitude, but also because of sin, then

[44] Hardy, *op. cit.,* p. 217.

Gregory surely leads us astray from the truth. At this point Augustine is right: "Every man from the commencement of his faith becomes a Christian *by the same grace* by which that man from the beginning became Christ." [45]

How far, nevertheless, was the human nature of Jesus independent of Godhood either in preparation for the fullness of time or in the fullness of time? We know that Jesus had weaknesses, ignorance, finitude and mortality. We know that he had real temptations of great depth and power. But did he sin? Did he have to sin in order to share our full, actual humanity? If sin is thought of as gross acts of misconduct we have no need to suppose Jesus guilty of sin. We cannot even argue from his submitting to baptism for the remission of sin that he was doing more than join a great prophetic movement "to fulfill all righteousness." Nor can we argue that he was a sinner from the fact that his own prayer contained petition for the forgiveness of trespasses or debts. Even his pleading that not he, but God alone, was good can witness to the purity of his own consciousness which, by being pure, was the more humble, acknowledging as right the great Jewish act of the worship of a God so qualitatively different from man that His full will went beyond man's capacity as far as the heaven is from the earth. On the other hand, Bible claims to the effect

---

[45] *A Treatise in the Predestination of the Saints,* chap. 31, in Schaff, *Nicene and Post-Nicene Fathers,* Vol. 5, p. 512. Cf: *"Ea gratia fit ab initio fidei suae homo quicumque Christianus, qua gratia homo ille ab initio suo factus est Christus"* (Migne, *Patrologia Latina,* V. 44, p. 982).

that Jesus was sinless have most weight for the literalist. Such language, too, can be ascribed to unreflective piety and adoration. However much we bend over backwards to soften the statements that involve the unsinlessness [46] of Jesus, the evidence of the New Testament seems to be on both sides.

Is there, then, a theological way to settle the question? Historically we cannot go beyond ignorance as far as certain knowledge goes, except for the registering of the fact that Jesus in the most natural and indirect instances seems to have been humbly conscious of sin before God. His identification with man in this respect was natural, unaffected and complete. Possibly we can say more. Sin is not to be thought of basically in terms of discrete acts, but as a relation to God. The definition in James to the effect that "whoever knows what is right to do and fails to do it, for him it is sin" (4:17) is a moralistic rendering of sin and not to be compared to the deeper definition of Paul that "whatsoever does not proceed of faith is sin" (Rom. 14:23). Sin is the *acceptance* of anxiety; fear is therefore the external sign of sin. Now watch the fact that Hebrews claims that for fear Jesus cried day and night unto him who was able to deliver him from death (Heb. 5:7). We have no right, of course, to take such a claim for literally reported history, but we can say that such a biblical assertion tallies to some real extent with the total account of his life. Perhaps the context of this experience was Messianic, Jesus being "made sin" in the

---

[46] I use this word because "sin*ful*ness" can hardly be applied to Jesus!

depth of his identification with both the will of God and the sins of his people.

Sin is "the set on self" which must be broken through by suffering. Jesus learned from the struggles of his moral conflicts, and through suffering accepted understanding and willing obedience. In this respect he was fully and gloriously human. In this sense the sinless God was present with the struggling Savior, as the victorious Godman, sharing the struggle and being "made sin" for us, but winning so amazingly over sin, as God and man organically united (that is as the Godman) that he became the first in the Kingdom, "the firstborn of many brethren," "the pioneer and perfecter of our faith." One of our greatest evangelists, who is himself something of a modern St. Francis, has suggested that Jesus must himself have been born again, and have given his injunction of man's necessity to be born again from personal experience. May we not also say that in some sense, if all human beings have to be born again in order to see the Kingdom of God, so did Jesus; or else the Son of God was never made fully man. Jesus, as a human being, was born again, and experienced rapture and new levels of acceptance by God. Jesus, on the other side of his human experience, was the one who first accepted Incarnation, who fulfilled conclusively both the presence and purpose of God and the nature and destiny of man. In him therefore came the fullness of time, first of all for himself and potentially for all men. Jesus went the shortest way that we know home to the Father. *Jesus was eternity's miracle of time.*[47] In him heaven and earth met and in him is the focus and turning point of all earthly history. Jesus knew sin, in some sense, as a minimal but real experience within his own life; and as a maximal experience outside himself because of his supreme concern for men. This conclusive concern which takes upon itself man's sin is the seal of the fullness of time, God's own inbreaking as decisive presence and power, to rescue man from his sinful plight.

Theologically Jesus did not save us from sin unless he assumed it within himself; and sin, not finitude, is precisely our deepest problem. Jesus was "made sin," however, not in the sense that God could ever sin, certainly not even in human form, but that the human nature of Jesus shared our whole history of alienation from God and accepted the anxiety connected with it which is the root reality of sin. *To remove Jesus from our sin categorically is to deny the Incarnation and to destroy its reality and power.*

God is precisely He who from His highest stoops to our lowest. He used the greatest power, Agape, to destroy from within our worst enemy, sin. The holiness of God is not only a withdrawal from sin, in the sense of intrinsic and inviolable

[47] "He lives among us in the identical conditions we live in. And proves that it can be done: that one can live a perfect Christian life in this world, in spite of darkness and death. He shows us that within the closed frontiers of this existence of ours one can lead a life that is entirely open towards God, entirely dependent upon God. He receives everything from God: from the Father and from himself as the Son" (Von Speyer, *The Word*, p. 139). The word "perfect" to me indicates a conclusively victorious life that finally broke through human history into the fullness of God by the presence and the power of God.

purity, but is also an outgoing purity questing to encounter sin and to slay it precisely by becoming the ally of the man who sins, against his own sins, and against the sins of man.

Incarnation is real. God became man! The Word became flesh! We need not deal with myth. Jesus as man was one of us. He knew our actual plight from within; but he was more than man, for God was in him reconciling the world unto Himself. God was there, not as in a dwelling, but organically united to, in and with man, constituting Jesus the Godman. God as Agape was present as the main Spirit of Jesus' life. God the Sinless entered our sinful world and by means of real human experience *from within* showed His power as the Sinless to defeat and to destroy sin, and along with sin, the ignorance, law and death which have come to be man's enemies because of sin. How can human pen phrase the most mysterious of all miracles: the creative and redemptive presence of God, as God, with man, as man, in the Incarnation!

Enhypostasia should safeguard the full humanity of Jesus and his full identification with actual human nature. We start, therefore, not with an unreal, but with a genuine human being in whom dwelt the Godhead bodily as the conclusive fulfillment of human nature and of history, actually in Jesus and potentially for all men. Jesus is the Godman who is the eternal purpose of God in the fullness of time. Therefore all things cohere in him.

When, however, did the hypostatic union take place? We cannot tell. Perhaps it is futile to analyze the event of the

Incarnation. The conclusive union, in any case, came early enough for Jesus to illustrate an Agape life, to die an Agape death, to rise from death as Agape everlastingly victorious. At what point the union became the basic fact of Jesus' life we cannot know, although it seems likely that it occurred before his baptism. After that he appears triumphant in his parables and sayings. *Enhypostasia,* nevertheless, stands for the solid fact that in spite of all victories and even transfiguration experiences the struggle remained through the wilderness temptations, Gethsemane and until his dying cry of desertion by God.

Can we say, in any case, that the struggle ceased with the Resurrection? Possibly, but we do not know. The basic union could last eternally, with victory now assured, and with companionship and participation in God beyond our understanding, and still leave room for further growth in the eternal disciplines and discipleships of God. *Enhypostasia,* therefore, stands also for the truth that human nature remains human after death and to all eternity. The human is transfigured by the heavenly and made at one with it, but never absorbed by it. Human life in the eternities may therefore see ever new meanings of *enhypostasia.* Such matters we can leave with complete confidence in the hands of God. In Jesus' case the union may have been so complete, in spite of Gethsemane and of Calvary, in one sense, and because of them, in another, that growth after death was merely the quiet walking of the Godman into the eternal realms of the Son of God. In his case the human past had only to discover ever more what in essence the Godward side of the Godman, the eternal Word, the everlasting Son of the Father, had always known. In the case of most men, however, who receive the Son as their basically guiding self, the process of growth beyond death may be far longer and basically different.

The important insistence of *enhypostasia,* however, is that Jesus remained the Godman forever, that he never shed his human nature, that he represents the fullness of time as God in man and man in God, neither by absorption, nor in separation, but as one organic, new creation of the uncreate and the create. Leo in his Tome once wrote that "every spirit which dissolveth Jesus is not of God, and this is Antichrist. Now what is to dissolve Jesus, but to separate the human nature from him." [48] Never to all eternity can this be done. A little later we shall try to show how these natures are related eternally and how the union affects men in history, but for now, we close this section on *enhypostasia* by insisting with Cyril that we cannot divide the hypostases in the one Christ after the union. In reality we must accept the Council of 681 which affirmed the two wills, in such a way not as to split the personality of Jesus, but as to assure his full humanity as well as his Godhood. We agree that "we will not therefore grant (the existence of) one natural operation of God and the creature, lest we should either raise up into the divine nature what is created, or bring down

[48] In Hardy, *op. cit.,* p. 367.

the pre-eminence of the divine nature into the place suitable for things that are made." [49] Rather by means of *anakephalaioosis,* and in the correct proportion and meaning of *anhypostasia* and *enhypostasia,* we see that the Incarnation is history's greatest truth and heaven's fullest revelation.

Revelation and redemption are one in Christ. God has come to save man by transforming him from within through his work in history and by participating Himself as man's chief partner in his own life. Our individuality must be lost by being truly fulfilled as well as guarded by our union and communion with Godhead. We can therefore affirm with Surjit Singh: "A revolution has taken place in the relation between God and man. You cannot separate man from God. The God-Man has significance for eternity. And, because this took place within time and history, it changes the value of time and historical existence." [50]

III. CATEGORIES FOR CHRISTOLOGY

We need a restatement of the cardinal truths of Christology in terms of modern categories. Ancient Christologies are couched in terms of substance philosophy. Such philosophy served its times, but is far from sacrosanct. In terms of substance philosophy the godhood was *ousia;* the personal distinctions within the godhood were a matter of *hypo-*

---

[49] "The Statement of Faith of the Third Council of Constantinople," *ibid.,* p. 384.
[50] *Preface to Personality,* p. 75.

stasis; [51] the relation between them was *perichoresis.* [52] There was only one "essence," and therefore only one God, whereas there were three persons, or intrinsic qualifications of substance, while these three persons, in turn, co-inhered among one another. God and man were then different substances in such a way that there could be no mutual co-inherence between them, except as God could permeate man because He is pure Spirit. The union between God and man took place in Jesus only by such permeation of an assumed humanity. Therefore Jesus is the unique enmanment of God in human history. Through him God is revealed and His redemptive purpose accomplished. The further question as to how God as Son could then permeate human nature in

[51] The Tome of Leo, for instance, indicates two natures or substances in Christ coming together in one person: two *physes* or *ousiae* in one *prosopon* or *hypotasis.* T. Torrance wants another word than *perichoresis* to express the relation between God and man since "where the natures differ the nature of the coinherence differs" (Minutes of the Commission of Faith and Order on Christ and His Church, discussion on my paper, "The Humanity of Jesus" at Oxford, England, August, 1956). Edmund Schlink also added at the same time that "to use the same word risks confusing the absolutely different relations between God and Jesus and God and us as adopted sons." My reply then was and remains that "the same God who is literally present in us was present in Jesus. The humanity of Jesus never ceases, and our own will not cease but be joined to his humanity; by grace we must come into the same relationship; and we are therefore literally joint heirs with Christ. This is my biggest departure from the tradition which says that God came only in the historic Christ."

[52] Gregory of Nyssa in effect expounded this relation of co-inherence or *circumcessio* in *Why We Believe in One God.* How different this concept becomes when delivered from the substance category, as for instance in G. B. Verity, *Life in Christ,* p. 199: "The price of co-inherence can be paid only by loving. There is no other way. The eternal relationship of the Trinity in Unity is the Co-inherence of Love: God so loved the world that He gave His Son to make Eternal Life possible for us: Christ gave Himself for us because He loves us—every one: we co-inhere with Him and with one another only in so far as we love as He loves."

general was never answered by the Fathers. Rather, they generally made Jesus the *only* point where God *in Himself* truly entered human history, thereby denying in fact the New Testament, and precluding, as we shall see, the development of any adequate Christian theology.

The trouble with substance theology, in spite of its appeal to common sense and especially to visual understanding, is that the categories are not basically relational. Substance theology is more inventory than explanation. It describes objects rather than accounts for their coming to be, their change, and their organic togetherness. Nor again can substance philosophy deal adequately with personal identity and social relations. Fundamentally substance philosophy is "a thing" language which has no unembarrassed place for persons as real in themselves, in fact as more real than the things which are created and pass away.

There is truth in substance philosophy which must be kept. The world that we know cannot be reduced to relations. Things are; and they are more than mere form of flux or patterns in process. Time is real and things are real as things. Events are made up of both process and reality at the same time. On the upper end of the scale, persons are also substances in the sense of natural occurrences. Substance philosophy therefore should stand guard against every idealism which explains away the stubborn actuality of creation. Men are part of natural creation as well as part of the spiritual world. Therefore substance philosophy has its rightful place in the economy of explanation. Nevertheless it falls short of being an adequate vehicle for the correct phrasing of Christology.[53]

Organismic categories are likewise inadequate. The distinctive and plenary relation between God and man is not biological, but theological. Life is important; and organism is a step nearer the decisive truth than mechanism. Organism fulfills mechanism. Those who have studied organisms know how mechanical is much of man's nature. A popular treatment of the relation between body and mind written by a group of generally competent scientists is Laslett's *The Physical Basis of Mind*. Chemical regulators and structural as well as organismic deficiencies affect mind drastically. No concept of freedom, for instance, is at all adequate that does not recognize the mechanical ingredients both in life as a whole, as we know it, and in mind. For this reason Wiener in *Cybernetics* can conclude that the mind when studied through the analogy of cybernetics is seen to be mechanical in nature. Function presupposes some structure; it presupposes at least that energy is dependably patterned in a certain describable and predictable manner for the time and purposes of investigation. Organism is thus mechanical in some of its aspects, but is more than and fulfills mechanism.

More and more we are coming to recognize that structure

[53] For instance, substance theology is presupposed by the following citation from Cyril: "If any one says that Jesus was energized as a man by the Word from God, and clothed with the glory of the Only-begotten, as being another besides him, let him be anathema" (Hardy, *op. cit.*, p. 354). The Word is never energy, but the self-subsisting, eternal, personal Spirit of holy Love.

is changed by function. Functional diseases can eventuate in structural changes. The model for biological and social sciences is increasingly recognized to be functional rather than structural in nature. Physiology takes the place quite naturally of mechanics and mathematics. Anatomy has its indispensable place, but to understand life and social relations the investigator needs to fill in his picture by recourse to the physiological model. In an organism there is, beyond its mechanical aspects, a purposive relation between the parts and the whole and among the parts. The eye directs the hand to feed the mouth to nourish the body as a whole. If one area of the brain is injured, other areas often take over the function of the destroyed part. There is mutual support and concern among the members of the body; and within, and for the whole; while the whole is more than any aggregate of parts and fulfills and aids their functions. An organism is also self-repairing and self-perpetuating in a way no machine is. It grows also by assimilation rather than by accretion. Function is thus a wider dimension than structure, and purpose alone gives adequate explanation for function in the organic world. Even from such mere suggestions as these it is evident that organismic philosophy is insufficient to do justice to Christological formulations. Lionel Thornton, for instance, in *The Incarnate Lord,* has reformulated the doctrine of Christ mainly in terms of organismic philosophy, particularly by means of the thought of A. N. Whitehead; but even his organismic philosophy falls short of categorical adequacy.

Beyond the organismic, moreover, lies the personalistic, which fulfills the organismic, in a way similar to the manner in which the organismic fulfills the mechanistic. No competent personalist, of course, would deny the predictable elements of experience which in this sense can be called mechanical; nor would he deny the organismic relations of purposiveness which precede and undergird the personal purpose. The personal realm, however, cannot be reduced to the organismic; and, much less, to the mechanistic. Personal life is characterized by free ideas and by deliberate choice. Animals cannot reflect, as far as we know, by the use of abstract ideas. To be personal involves transcendence of the actual world by means of free ideas and the making of choices based on a deliberate review of possibilities. Personal life has entered the dimension of symbolic thinking, of picturing realities behind, and more than, the figures through which they are conceived of and contacted.

The personal realm is therefore also moral on a new level. A person can weigh possible choices, not only in terms of future pain and pleasure, but in terms of right and wrong. He can also discover a realm of moral reality that affects his inner self and that is intrinsic to the larger world. The personal level is thus characterized by rational and moral choice with regard to both self-knowledge and the understanding of truth and right. It is the level of freedom and responsibility. At its highest, it attains to the personal and prophetic consciousness of God and His rule. In the light of God, this life is seen to be only one part of His full rule, and man has actually come to believe in life after death. High religion has lifted personalism into an understanding and acceptance of life eternal as God's purpose for creation.

Christological formulations on this level are intrinsically more adequate than on the previous two. Such is certainly the case if the personal category is made inclusive of the other two. The temptation is, however, to use only the distinctively personal category, employing, at the most, the mechanical and the organismic only insofar as they are included within the individual experience while neglecting the intrapersonal realities and relations. Personalities, to be sure, are held together from within in terms of self-consciousness, of self decision, of memory linkages, of aims at future satisfaction and of self-experience generally. *Personalities do not overlap as personalities.* They are social in origin and social in content of knowledge. They are social with regard to much of their reference or attention.

What makes a person himself, however, is his stark individuality, his aloneness, his self-being. Consider St. Thomas' definition: *Persona individua est, in se subsistens, ab aliquis separata.* Here we have threefold incommunicability. A person is not merely a substance or an organism, although there is substantive sameness and organismic wholeness within his life. A person is a distinct unity of experience, of self-reference, of inexchangeable feelings. Whitehead's attempt to say that there are no distinctions between private and public feelings was misdirected. There are private feelings which are had uniquely and cannot ever be experienced by anyone else exactly as they are experienced by the person himself.[54] A personalistic Christology has therefore real capacity for Christ as a person. It has ample means for expressing the moral and the rational elements in Christology. In a world of persons confronting one another, of laws to be kept and of love to be lived, the personalist category is pre-eminently useful and so far true.[55] Its great expression is Hebrew religion. It can pull out all stops on the organ of explanation and describe for us a majestic, living, personal God, and men as made in His image and for His love.

For worship and ethics the personal level may, therefore, be our most adequate dimension.[56] Its lines are clear and

[54] Whitehead's category of "absolute self-enjoyment," the third phase of the concrescence of each occasion of experience, analytically more than chronologically, ought to involve such denial of public feelings as damage the integrity of the private, personal self—although his total emphasis is also needed.

[55] Cf. Toynbee's observation that "the play of Intellect and Will is the only movement known to Man that appears to be unquestionably non-recurrent" (*An Historian's Approach to Religion*, p. 10).

[56] Consider Thomas Torrance's insistence that "the Chalcedonian Christology was written on its knees; it comes out of the worship and adoration of the Church and therefore the mystery of Christ occupies a great place" (Minutes of the Oxford discussion of Faith and Order Commission, August, 1956). He feels that to attempt to penetrate the mystery of the relation of Christ's two natures is to tear aside the mystery. Edmund Schlink joined him: "We all hesitate here, before absurdity or mystery. I think the mystery of the Chalcedonian formula does not come from the formula itself, which is only a doxological ending—but which, however, presupposes the act of redemption as a vicarious redemption. To all the Fathers who prepared the way for this, from Athanasius to Cyril and Leo, what mattered was the mystery of vicariousness, the question of how Christ was made divine. At that time the idea of divinization was not so frightening as it is to-day. If the mystery of vicariousness had been recognized as the centre of Christology, we should no longer be afraid of its modernistic misinterpretation to look at it like that. . . . It is obvious that, considering the doxological ending, one cannot explain the soteriological. In theological thinking there are one-

convincing within the confines of its explanatory and religious limits. The only place where it fails necessarily is in the realm of Incarnation. The personal level can and does develop strongly the aspect of confrontation and of moral union in Christology but it cannot understand and accept the doctrine of actual co-inherence or co-subjects. The doctrine of the Incarnation must, therefore, be formulated in its full meaning on a level still higher than the personal. From the perspective of personalism, "co-subjects" is Nestorianism so-called, and to be condemned; on this level, co-subjects keep Jesus and Christ distinct, a false position which Irenaeus rejected already and after him all high formulators of Christology. To speak of co-subjects on the level of personalism is to deny the unity of the historic Jesus

---

way streets where you cannot turn back. The Chalcedonian formula cannot explain the historical life of Christ. This is generally accepted today. . . . It is possible from the Synoptics to get to Chalcedon, it is inevitable; but from there you cannot go back to the Gospel. That is not even the intention of Chalcedon. . . . Put the two statements together that 'God was in Christ' and 'God has been made sin, who knew no sin,' and then you reach the point of vicariousness as a means, and doxological statements result—but you cannot do it the other way round, because then you would lose yourself in speculation" (*ibid.*).

My reply is that if Chalcedon is needful mystery in the sense of being impervious to explanation, I respect its vision of insight and thank God. If, however, Chalcedon is actually a definitive statement of the God-man relation that most fully illumines life and its meaning, then we cheat ourselves and the world by ruling out of court this meaning before giving it a chance to be heard. I believe that the fact and principle of Incarnation are central to all life and history, that the Christian faith is indeed the Gospel of truth. I believe that Christ is at the center of reality and thought and I am eager to capture all thought for Him who is the truth. The New Testament has ample grist for a full Christology. As a matter of fact, it is refreshing to come across Berkouwer's assertion, with which I agree, that "Chalcedon is not as rich as that Scriptural fullness on which the church, in its preaching, is continually allowed to draw" (*op. cit.*, p. 96).

and thus to fall short of Chalcedonian correctness. D. M.
Baillie might well call the biblical affirmation "It is no longer
I who live, but Christ who lives in me; and the life which
I now live" (Gal. 2:20)—a paradox, for looking at it from
our ordinary personalistic point of view we have in such
an indwelling of Christ a split or divided personality or some
phenomenon of pathological possession.

When, however, we move up to the level of spiritual
reality, we dwell no longer in the realm of paradox, but in
the land of true explanation.[57] Before going on to develop
Christology from the spiritual level, however, let us take a
long look at the following affirmation from the point of
view of substance philosophy. The nature of substance is to
be itself, as substance philosophy is correctly interpreted;
thus Godhood and manhood are qualitatively distinct, separated by an unbridgeable gulf. Incarnation, on such a basis,
becomes a sheer miracle wrought by God, for two qualitatively distinct substances can never be organically joined,
but held together only within the special creation of a unique
personality. Outside this miracle of Incarnation God is
never present in history personally and He is present there
only in disguise as the miracle of time. Jesus therefore
becomes the unrepeatable "Christian moment" rather than
the universal "Socratic occasion."[58] Truth is bound up with
him inseverably and uniquely in such a way that God never

[57] This fact broke in even on Søren Kierkegaard in 1848 when he turned
to direct writing, accepting Christianity as "complete clarity."
[58] This will be discussed more fully in chap. 4.

is thus joined to anyone else. Revelation and redemption are through Jesus, in the fullness of time; they are through him who was God in human flesh for our salvation. Through this miracle and through this miracle alone God then draws near to men. He subsequently comes into men, not as God, but as the Christ, the Godman. The humanity of Jesus becomes the avenue of His approach to men. Therefore there can be no salvation, *ever,* apart from this one saving Name, for here and here alone heaven touched earth and eternity transformed time.

Barth, for instance, stresses the humanity of Jesus and objects to all attempts to know Jesus no longer as man, for the manhood of Jesus is, in fact, the very door that God has opened by his Self-coming into history. Christology has been developed along such lines as these largely, perhaps, because of the substance philosophy within which the Early Fathers had to think, but also, to be sure, because of both the tendency to make myths and the genuine humility and adoration of simple piety. The Bible was written within such an atmosphere, and the marvel is not that such a Christology becomes more and more prominent in the later strands, but far rather that so much of authentic tidings of the genuine humanity of Jesus and his real relation with us before God actually remain. Imagine the biblical writers actually allowing Jesus to say: "Why do you call me good? No one is good but God alone" (Mark 10:18).

Organismic philosophy, again, which is mostly modern, finds Jesus to be the fullness of time in terms of the decisive novelty of union between God and man. Jesus becomes the firstborn among many brethren in the unique sense of the constitutive relation, in the fullness of time, between God and man, or as the union of God and man. Organismic philosophy consequently has the capacity beyond all substantive formulations to describe the organic relationships between God in Jesus as the Christ and between God in us as new creatures in Christ. Organismic philosophy can therefore be of real help in the formulation of Christology. On the other hand, organismic philosophy, taken from within its own perspectives and presuppositions, does not have an adequate understanding of God as the supernatural Creator, Controller, Redeemer and Fulfiller of the world. In this view God is not the self-sufficient Reality who freely creates at will because He loves, but the mental pole of a process of creativity. Process becomes the center of explanation and organic relations are defined as purposive for process. The organic stress is good, but its continuity and coextensiveness with process need the metaphysical discontinuity of the personal, and, even more so, of the spiritual.

We have already shown how the personal by not allowing the overlapping of selves precludes any adequate formulation of Incarnation, but how, on the other hand, it fulfills what is true in the substantive and the organismic view of reality. The following discussion will be devoted to showing how the category of the Spirit is the most inclusive and adequate of all the categories of God as Agape to formulate

Christology. The spiritual category does justice to the main criteria of Christology: the oneness of God, the true deity and humanity of Jesus, and the genuineness and unity of his personality. Before we start this discussion it will be well to keep in mind that the clue to Incarnation is *perichoresis* or co-inherence.

There is but one God. He is *Spirit*. The *form* of Spirit is personal; [59] the *content* of Spirit is *Love*. There is but one uncreate eternal Spirit, the Father almighty who creates because He is Love. At the ground of the universe and the universes is creative Being whose very nature is to turn the exhaustless abyss of non-being into meaningful becoming. Spirit is the capacity to be oneself and yet to create what is other than self; Spirit is the ability to be in oneself and yet to communicate with what is not self; Spirit is the power

---

[59] Something essential to the Christian faith is lost if we say with Tillich that God is "transpersonal in power and mystery" *The Biblical Faith and the Search for Ultimate Reality,* p. 84). Or with Grensted that "we are on safer ground if we regard personality [in God] as the potentiality of personal relationships" (*op. cit.,* p. 220). Here H. H. Farmer (*Religion and Revelation*) needs to tell us that any framing of the Christian faith that in its ultimate reality, *its very ontology,* has God less than personal is both false and inadequate. But I differ with Farmer; since God is also impersonal, or since His being as Spirit, is more than personal in the sense of its inclusive operation and manifestations, God cannot be defined solely as Personality. But the personal category of Agape is the definitive albeit not the most inclusive category. If only instead of having Being itself ultimate, or the "Personal-Itself" that is only the ground of personal being, Tillich could agree with Farmer in making the personal an ultimate category, effectively though not exclusively! Love is always personal at the highest we know. Suppose then Tillich took metaphysically seriously his own statement: "Therefore, we need not only an ethics of love, but, following Augustine, also an ontology of love"! (*op. cit.,* p. 69).

thus to transcend self by creative society and communication. There is but one God and they who worship Him must worship the Spirit in spirit and in truth, calling Him our Father who is in heaven, for He is Love and can be known only by those who love. The preceding sentences contain reference to all the major components of God, if we may thus speak, and precisely those which are made central in the New Testament. This Spirit, Father, Love is also through and through holy in His inviolate character of Light and in His flaming opposition to sin as a devouring Fire.

There is only one Spirit who is Father-Love. The order is important: the Spirit is a Person who is Love. If the personal category is made ultimate, we may have a trinitarian formula of Father, Love and Spirit. We have seen, however, that if we start with the personal category as ultimate, we arrive at a doctrine not of Incarnation, but only of confrontation and of moral union. If we start with Spirit, on the other hand, we have a more inclusive category of explanation of reality as a whole, and *one in which Incarnation becomes central to this understanding.*

The Spirit, then, has worked broodingly over the void to call forth order ever since the beginnings of creation. As the personal response to the Spirit developed there began to be encounter. Encounter is symbolized by the alienation of the original human beings, occasioned by a tree of temptation in the midst of their existence. The encounter became cumulative, developing a deep and long history of struggle with

God, of hiding from Him behind clothes and bushes; and yet also of walking with Him. At the same time there developed a history of the Spirit within prophetic personalities, as a penetrating fire burning in their bones. The Hebrew genius, being mostly prophetic in nature, recognized chiefly the personal and the ethical sides to religion. The Hebrew people, to be sure, had their kind of philosophy, whatever be said about it, but their philosophy was much more one of living encounter and obedience than of explanation and understanding how God came to man and how He operated in nature. The Greeks had much more of an explanatory bent. Largely under their influence men like Philo evolved a *logos* doctrine. This *logos* understanding is not one of external encounter as much as one of interpenetration, of co-inherence. Out of *both the Hebrew and the Greek backgrounds* came the Christian understanding of the Incarnation of the living Personal God. Such a doctrine combines both streams and no reformulation of Christology can avoid this fact because both streams contain valid and necessary insights into the ultimate nature of things. The nature of God and His relation to the world need to be interpreted in terms of both Spirit and Person, and of both as expressing Love.

There is but one personal Spirit who is God. There can therefore be legitimate worship of only one God, as the Jews and the Moslems have stubbornly maintained. On the level of encounter there is only one God to encounter, the Father of our Lord, Jesus Christ, the God of Abraham, Isaac and

Jacob. Incarnation is also true, however, because the very nature of Spirit is to co-inhere. God created man such that he can never find fulfillment apart from the personal Presence of God as Spirit. The history of encounter and of interpenetration up to the coming of the Christ was a living, true growth based on an *interactive* experience of encounter and interpenetration. God became known as one, living, personal, righteous, redeeming Love, at the highest pinnacles of Old Testament thought, but only in Jesus Christ did this ultimate nature of truth come to conclusive clarity and to consummate enactment. Both these streams of Spirit and Love are organically interdependent and fulfilled only as they pass through dialectic tension to dynamic co-operation within personal experience.

In Jesus, by the supreme initiative of God, encounter and interpenetration reached the climax wherein eternity fulfilled time.[60] After him, as far as he is understood and accepted, history is no longer a matter of search, but of making him Lord as the true representative of God, because he was actually the presence of God in and with the presence of

[60] This interpenetration is always a matter of God's initiative. It is primarily characteristic of the nature of God, but it should also be understood in its incarnational sense as the answer to the nature of the hypostatic union. A citation from Verity is helpful: "The word *perichoresis* itself is not found in the writings of the fathers of the Early Church before the seventh century, when Maximus the Confessor used it of the two natures in Christ, the Human and the Divine, and then in the sense of the 'reciprocity of action'— e.g., the relation, at the moment of utterance, between the sound of a spoken word and its meaning—they are distinct and yet both the 'word.' Pseudo-Cyril used it in this sense of the Nature of Christ: the human nature of Christ, he taught, does not permeate through the Divine Nature, but the Divine permeating through the Human bestows upon it an ineffable co-inherence with Itself" (*op. cit.,* p. 189).

man. He was God enmanned. He was the Son of God and the Son of Man, revealing both God and man and making effective man's atonement as the Godman's triumphant suffering over law, sin and death. In Jesus, as far as the basic reconciliation and fulfillment of human history goes, the supreme initiative of God met the supreme response of man. God came as Son, not as another personality besides Himself, but as the personal Spirit of Love who God is, to fulfill the life of Jesus and of all mankind.

The new personality, the Godman, is now neither a divine personality besides God, some second God, nor is he any longer a human personality merely enhanced by some spiritual infilling, but a whole new species, a whole new creation, a whole new begetting, wherein the personality is actually the Godman, the *perichoresis* of God and man, *maintaining distinction on the level of encounter*—so that Jesus could pray "My God and your God"— while also, at the same time, effecting a metaphysical union without division or separation of spirits—so that Jesus could truly say literally in the most important of all categories: "The Father and I are one." Thus Jesus is of both God and man, but more properly the Godman, not "a third species" besides God and man, but the new Being of God and man, a new *relation*.

The Virgin Birth is correctly used only as a symbol for the fact of the miraculous conception of the Son of God: God as Incarnate Spirit comes only from God as Eternal Spirit.

(This *ultimately* important truth must not be reduced to and spoiled by the biological category.) The finite spirit can in no way bridge the chasm between God and man, between the Uncreate and the create. This is a truth of substance philosophy. But the infinite Spirit, on every level of its activity, can be related to and work within the human organism. This is a truth of organismic philosophy. Yet beyond the organic interactions lies the truth of a distinct personality as self-decision and self-experience. Without encounter, struggle, growth and moral union there can be no Incarnation that goes beyond pantheism. The fact that the divine Person is reflected in the human person, necessitating challenge and response, stands guard over the reality of creation and of human personality. Yet on the personalistic level of understanding there is no interpenetration of Spirit and spirit that evolves into a new creation, not only through acceptance of moral and spiritual goals but through the actual co-drives and co-operation which eventuate in the new creation of the Godman. For the fullness of time we need the category of the Spirit in which Jesus is actually the firstborn of all creation, both on the side of the original creation through the eternal Word and through the new creation by "the Virgin Birth." The Virgin Birth, if the expression is to be used at all, belongs to the highest category of the Spirit. The Virgin Birth then stands for the fact, beyond any question of physical conception, that Jesus is Revelation, Redemption and Resurrection only because his constituent nature is very God of very God, a determining relation through which alone the humanity of Jesus could be fulfilled.[61]

The Atonement, similarly, is possible primarily because of the Godhood of Jesus, requiring, nevertheless, the full co-operation, and indeed fulfillment of the manhood, through the real Person who combined both natures livingly and triumphantly. The Godhood became organically the fulfillment of all genuine human needs, in the ultimate perspective, in such a way that man through the presence of God became genuinely victorious over law, sin and death *within his own experience.* God's assumption of the full normal humanity was necessary for man's deliverance from his actual pedagogical nature, over against God, anxious and sinful, and for a new being in God, fearfree and sinless. Only the altogether holy God could overcome sin. He who is Spirit and Love overcomes sin in freedom, offering man a living way through His flesh. The All-holy identifies Himself with man in his very situation, "becomes sin" for him, participates in his temptations and lives as a new power in man in order that man may now conquer, not as God nor as man, but as the destined Godman, for whom creation is made in the first place. Such are the vicariousness and substitution

[61] It is well to recall the Fifth Ecumenical Council (553), that anathematized anyone who tries to "introduce one nature or substance from the Godhead and flesh of Christ" (Hardy, *op. cit.,* p. 380). While being conclusively interpenetrated and obedient to the divine Will and Presence, the full humanity remained in Jesus. His humanity was fulfilled by the person of God in him. Emil Brunner's distinction between the person and the personality of Jesus in *The Mediator* is most cogent. The personality is more than the person for here the humanity is included in dynamic interpenetrative, regulative fulfillment. The personality of Jesus was first fully human in the normative sense because it was first rightly and fulfillingly related to God as Agape.

in which the All-holy identifies Himself with man and through participation in human affairs gives His life unto death until the power of Love becomes a stream of light, healing and immortality through which man is delivered from the curse of law, sin and death. Forgiveness becomes not only free acceptance, but the free acceptance of God's love which organically involves the concern and the power for restoration of righteousness and the re-creation of the moral order according to the original pattern of God's eternal purpose in Christ Jesus. The power of the law is broken through, abolished by being fulfilled, not as law in itself, or as some objective realm outside God, but as the life *in* God which is the meaning and purpose of law.

The Resurrection, too, depends on God's being in Jesus, not separately from his humanity but with his humanity forever, in such a way that the Godman could not be held by death. His actual appearance to his disciples fulfilled a historic purpose, but his rising over death was an eternal necessity. Jesus rose not as Spirit nor as spirit, but as the Godman, combining both in the genuine personality of a new creation. As such he was first-born from the dead. Whether others were resuscitated before him is of no moment. Jesus rose the first-born from the dead in the full sense of death and resurrection. He was the first in the Kingdom over whom death could have no control. Jesus was raised to the right hand of God, being forevermore *of* God, but without ever losing his humanity. In this sense we are joint-heirs with Christ. In this fact lies our hope. This is the Gospel of Jesus and the Resurrection which constituted the heart of the original proclamation. The Resurrection is no isolated event, but the place where all the roads of God's purpose run together for our salvation. God who is eternal Love here became victorious over death as Spirit, fulfilling spirit in the victory of the new person of Christ and in the new persons in Christ. The Godman, eternally in God and with God, being of God and God, brings to fruition the whole creation, being in man and with man, being of man and man. The Resurrection as fact and history, and as symbol and prophecy, is the central fact of the Christian faith, presupposing both Incarnation and Atonement.

God incarnate is Spirit, the personal Word from one personal God who is Love. Man is spirit, a human personality dominated in himself and his circumstances by self-need and self-reference. God is Agape and man is eros. All Agape is of God and is Spirit. Such love can be shed abroad in man's hearts only by the Spirit, known to man through the Person-event of encounter and co-inherence which is the Christ-deed of God in the fullness of time. Incarnation of Love cannot come as one would send a package. Love comes down into human history not as a substance. Nor does God send another separate personality to earth, as though there were more than one personal God! Love is sent as Spirit and as Encounter, through a preparation of human history and through personal decision. God became incarnate in Jesus by coming Himself into human life and into human history, by coming as the Agape who alone fulfills and transforms eros as the fullness of time. Such Incarnation requires God's supreme initiative and man's conclusive response, eventuating in a Person, the Godman, the central event of history, wherein the drive to self, desire for others and emptiness for God [62] is transformed into the acceptance of self in God, into the true community of the Spirit that is the real Church, and into the communion with God, on the personal level, that rises to true union with God on the spiritual level.

The Incarnation is thus the original fact of man's true history. God here declares His eternal faithfulness to man by His own presence and power. The Godman becomes the rock of revelation, the stream of redemption, and the power of resurrection. The Godman becomes the mediator of the true God who both relates Himself through the mediation of history in the fullness of time and encounters each person as a self and enters him as the fulfilling Spirit.[63] Jesus relates us vertically to God and also horizontally to each other. The Godman is the prototype and the reality of God's eternal pattern and presence in man. Apart from such a pattern and such a presence of God as has been declared in Jesus and through him, there can be no salvation. Such a pattern and such a relation to God, on the very contrary, define salvation

[62] In a sense we can use Hendry's insight in this context. "In this way it seems possible for Christian theology to recognize the element of truth in the Platonic doctrine of *anamnesis* and the description of the spirit's activity as *eros;* for *eros,* as the child of *poros* (plenty) and *penia* (poverty), represents the longing for a lost fullness" (*The Holy Spirit in Christian Theology,* p. 117).

[63] "It is the paradox of grace that God in descending to man, does not *un*-man him, as we might expect, seeing that He is God; by choosing to become man, He affirms his manhood, He subjects Christology to anthropology" (*ibid.,* p. 113).

and afford the opportunity for its being effected.[64] The Godman relation is "the Christian moment" apart from which no man can ever become right with God. The manhood of Jesus was historically indispensable for God's revelation, redemption and conquest of death. Spirit could save spirit only by fulfilling man, because *Spirit is God as Love.*[65] The Spirit who is Love enters vicariously into man's sinful state and frees him, from within, by means of man's cooperation. The Spirit who is Love conquers death by His unconquerable union with mortal man.

Yet the same Son of God's love, the same Christ, defined as the fulfilling union of God and man, must be in us also. We must have the same Spirit and the same mind, knowing Christ no longer as man, but knowing Christ rather as the Savior of men who introduces them into the mystery of the Love of God, into communion with Him and into the fulfilling co-inherence of the Spirit. The Godman becomes the occasion and the power for the Godmen who are born neither of blood nor of the will of the flesh nor of the will of man, but of God. Thus, by means of God's coming from eternity into time as the fullness of time we shall ourselves

[64] Even if God has made a living Way to Himself once for all we must *walk in it* as well as choose it. There is therefore a danger in statements like Hendry's, "In the assumption that the mission of Christ is transmissible to his disciples, there is an implicit denial of the completeness and the finality of the work of Christ and with that, a loss of its evangelical character; for what makes the gospel truly gospel is that fact that it is finished. God's decisive deed for the salvation of the world is done once for all and nothing needs to be added to it" (*ibid.,* p. 57).

[65] "The intention of the Synoptics is to present the life of Jesus as one wholly possessed and directed by the Spirit" (*ibid.,* pp. 18-19).

find the power to become sons of God. What the final relation of the concrete God-deed in a particular human being bears to all men past and future, and to all beings in unimaginable existences, we cannot tell. For us, what this Christ-deed should mean is its acceptance and our living within its power for salvation.

We have barely suggested some aspects of the importance of the manhood of Jesus. Only God saves. But the God who is Love saves only within the experiences of those whom He has created for the free acceptance of His love. God therefore saves as the Godman. For this reason it is of utmost importance that we affirm, at the same time, both the genuineness of the full humanity of Jesus and the victorious presence of God in his humanity. We are saved through no earthly wisdom, growth or obedience. We are saved only by means of the full love of God through its whole extension of purpose and operation. We are saved because God entered into our foolishness, our arrested development and disobedience, letting the Son of Man learn obedience through his suffering and letting the Son of God find the genuine victory of love by his conquering through such suffering man's fiercest enemies both within and without. With some understanding of the meaning of Incarnation and with some touch of gratitude to God for His great salvation, we can affirm as the central Christian fact and as the mainspring of our lives that God was in Christ reconciling the world unto Himself. God became the Godman in Jesus Christ that He might make us Godmen eternally.

III

THE ATONEMENT

THE atonement is central to Christology. This fact is true
for far deeper reasons than Christianity's being a religion
of salvation. Creation itself is for the sake of the kind of
freedom that is meaningless apart from sin. Creation is in
order that man may become estranged from God and reconciled to Him. Not only ignorance and immaturity but even
alienation from the God we know and can know, is part of
the divine plan. God wants man to be authentically real
and free in order that with mature insight and willing love
he may accept God as Father and Friend. For this reason
the Lamb is "slain before the foundation"; the Cross is
central not only to history but to the eternal plan of God,
to the eternal purpose which He purposed in Christ Jesus
our Lord.

The atonement, therefore, is central to revelation also.
God reveals through the Cross His love unto death. The
Cross is the final seal and sign of His self-giving love,
unconditional in its redemptive perseverance. It is our "being

rooted in love by the blood of Christ." [1] The Cross is the guarantee of the basis and bond of our eternal life in God. The atonement is therefore the content of revelation whereby creation becomes intelligible. The atonement is in principle and power the heart of God for sinful man, not as a mysterious stranger who comes to a foreign land but as the very life of One who comes to His own, whether or not they receive Him.

To make the atonement central to creation and revelation is not necessarily to make law, or even holiness, ultimate to the nature of reality. To conceive of atonement basically in terms of law or holiness is, in fact, to make law or holiness ultimate to reality. Rather, atonement in its ultimate reach is reconciliation. It is an effecting and a restoring of community. It is the establishment of fellowship. To be sure, law is instrumental and holiness cannot be slighted in the least. God is holy and the atonement presupposes His perfect righteousness. But creation, revelation and atonement are all means to man's salvation, to his perfect acceptance of God's righteousness and to his unqualified enmanment within God's perfect communion and community. Thus atonement is central to creation and revelation without being central to eternal reality. Atonement is central to the God-man, to the Incarnate Word, without being central to the heavenly Christ and to His Church. Atonement is central to the ways of God on earth, even if not in heaven. Even in

[1] *Letters of Ignatius: Smyrnaeans,* in Richardson, ed., *Early Christian Fathers,* p. 113.

heaven, however, there is no heavenly community apart from the grace of redemption, the center and fulfillment of creation and revelation.

Many theologians have, in fact, started their Christology with the atonement. The works of Christ declare him, maintained the Reformers. Melanchthon's *Hoc est Christum cognoscere, beneficia ejus cognoscere* has had a long and honorable history.[2] Nevertheless, we must never thus separate knowledge from being, and works from reality. The very nature of God as Agape, the personal Spirit who is holy Love, is revealed precisely at its deepest in the atonement. To be sure, the atonement is never carried out apart from the resurrection. Only because Christ rose victoriously over sin, law and death have we a living way to full salvation. The atonement presupposes and is completed only by the resurrection. Easter gives full power to Good Friday, which, in turn, gives full meaning to Christmas.

The atonement, however, may be the most offensive of all doctrines to modern man. Or possibly prayer may be more offensive, insofar as faith in prayer makes the primary presupposition of a God who acts in human history. Man dreads the reality of God's presence, unless, of course, he has come to terms with Him. Prayer is offensive, therefore, mostly to those who crave to believe that there is no God at all before whom they must stand. But if prayer is thus offensive because it requires personal decision as to the reality of the living God, what of the atonement that shows us that the God

[2] Introduction to his *Loci theologici.*

who draws nigh is the God of the Cross? How much more offensive to the man who seeks self-security and who wants to rely on his own righteousness is the God of the Cross? As Bultmann has said: "By giving up Jesus to be crucified, God has set up the Cross for us." [3] The atonement is a scandal to us because the Cross is our deepest dread; natural man flees fastest from the total Cross that is offered not only *for* us but also *to* us.

Much difficulty, of course, is not with the real understanding of atonement. Men rightly dread "stuffy" theology. Honest men cannot swallow theology like medicine, holding their noses and gulping hard. Theologians have all too often and all too much substituted clichés for reality, and ingrown orthodoxies for the straight line of the Gospel. We must look, consequently, at some unreal theories before we advance to the real one. If Christology, particularly on the subject of atonement, loses full touch with actual human lives and problems, to light up, to relieve, and to enable men to find fuller integrity, reality, and newness of life, such theology is poison. We need clean, shining thinking, freeing us in mind and spirit. Genuine atonement is life seen at its deepest meaning and saved at the center of its reality. No doctrine of the atonement is true that, if accepted, fails radically to affect for the better personal and social life.

The Christian faith teaches at its very heart, in some sense, "substitutionary," vicarious or representative atonement. The

[3] "New Testament and Mythology," in Bartsch, *Kerygma and Myth,* p. 36.

atonement, somehow, is what God has done for us in our stead and what we could not do for ourselves. The atonement signifies and summarizes what God has done for us in Christ to remove our sins from us and to set us right with Himself, thereby letting us attain our truest and most satisfactory selfhood. The atonement centrally is God's being in Christ to reconcile the world to Himself. We should stress at the outset that the atonement is inclusive and conclusive rather than exclusive and external. Atonement is illustrative as well as actual in Jesus Christ. As in the case of the Incarnation, incarnation is God's incoming and indwelling in total humanity to fulfill His final purpose, so the Atonement on Calvary includes God's general atonement from the first incipient, redemptive act in human history to the final consummation of redemption at the end of human time.

Some of the theories of the atonement, as we have said, are immoral and unreal. They are mainly of three kinds: (1) those that presuppose that God is not through and through Agape; (2) those that forfeit the needed place of law; and (3) those that prevent or thwart man's true freedom and self-being.

There are doctrines that separate, in effect, the Father from the Son in such a way that a shadow is cast on the character of God the Father. It is often forgotten that "the Son" is God the Son with whom the Father is fully present, doing the work even of reconciliation. There must be no split between the Father and the Son either in character or in ultimate being. The only begotten Son is begotten in eternity, is with God, and is God from the beginning. The "only" refers not to the humanity of the historic Jesus, but to the eternal Son who is eternally begotten in the bosom of the Father. Consequently some old manuscripts speak of the only begotten God (John 1:18). God himself came as Son, the only true God who from eternity so loved the world that He sent His only begotten Son. From God alone comes salvation through His Son, begotten and not made before all ages. This God, as this Son, is the reconciler, the atoner.

From the manner in which "for Jesus' sake" is often used in church worship one would think it was a magic formula to make God do something that He otherwise would or could not do. Any doctrine, however, that implies by its ascription to Jesus, or to the Son, that God is not in His own nature and eternally the same reconciler and of the same character and concern as the Son is a false theory of atonement. Peter Taylor Forsyth has well said that the Cross does not procure but bestows grace. The fact is that God Himself has made a new and living way through His Son through which we are saved in actuality, but God Himself is the only and sufficient savior. He need not be placated. The Christian faith repudiates, at its inmost center and by its very nature, the claim that God is too holy to behold or to deal redemptively with sin. Instead it proclaims that God Himself enters our humanity and our history to take on Himself our sins and to bear them for us in order that, loving the sinners all the way to His own death as human son,[4] He might separate the sin from the sinner and thus make peace by His blood.

The second kind of inadequate theory of the atonement is the kind that forfeits the rightful and necessary place of the law. Law is no second god to be served, but law, in the sense of righteousness or of right relations, is an intrinsic element of reality, and if we may speak reverently, of the nature of God. Sin is serious because law can never be by-passed. It can be abolished as a demand over against us only by being fulfilled. If we can never fulfill the perfect law of righteousness in our own strength and wisdom we are always under the condemnation of the law. God requires such fulfillment not because it is impossible nor in order to humiliate us. He requires of us the perfect fulfillment of a humanly unfulfillable law in order that we might find in Him and through Him our true selves and the power we need to fulfill the law. Atonement is the gateway to such fulfillment of the law. It is the finding the righteousness of Christ that is our own true righteousness of life through our right relation to God. Law, which is right relation to God and with all else, is fulfilled only when God becomes the governing center and reality of our lives.

Any theory therefore that sells sin short and weighs law light is false. Many doctrines of the atonement, in effect, speak of the abolition of the law and of a forgiveness of sin which is not only a restoration of fellowship but the acquit-

---

[4] If such an assertion seems to separate the eternal Son from the historic, we have to face the fact that the Godman can die but not God. Further explanation of this fact will be made in the next chapter.

ting of the consequences of sin. The consequences of sin go on even when guilt is forgiven. The relations are not made right by mere forgiveness. The murderer, when he repents, is forgiven, but the one murdered remains dead. The man who cuts off his left hand in anger with himself, even in a frenzy of guilt feelings, can be forgiven by God and restored to Christian fellowship, but his hand is not therefore restored to him. Equally real, or more so, are mental, social and spiritual consequences that remain even when forgiveness is complete. God in and with men restores wrong relations and renews right ones, the claim of the law, insofar as there is re-creation of the false and the wronged past. Sin is serious in the depth of payment that it exacts in terms of human suffering and creative toil. Many doctrines are constructed with a view wherein God could disregard the righteous demands of the law or could pay for sin externally to some cosmic person or force rather than assume in himself, *within humanity and within history,* man's sins and shortcomings, and thus pay for, cancel from within, and make new and right, *from within,* what was wrong and broken.

One such false explanation, wrong to the point of crudity, was expounded from the pulpit in a large Southern city. The preacher explained that "Jesus was the Ticket Fixer." He pointed out how sooner or later most people get a ticket for speeding and how good it is to have some friend on the police force who "fixes" the ticket, making it unnecessary for the violator of the traffic law to appear in court. Jesus, the preacher explained, is the only one who can make us go "scot free." Even if it was presupposed by the preacher that Jesus had himself enough money to pay for all fines, so that the law was not by-passed but fulfilled by someone else, the very purpose of the law is in effect destroyed. Such an offer of "fixing" is an incentive to disregard a needed law rather than an inducement to remain under the law in order to fulfill it. If this is what is meant by "Jesus paid it all," we have in fact a most immoral theory both of law and of atonement. Transgression is far more serious than to be curable by such an external work. Sin has to be broken within the law and in relation to it. The law has to be fulfilled by the violator. He must obtain the will and the power to live within the law or within right relations.

The third kind of immoral and inadequate doctrine further clarifies why the other two were false. The third immoral doctrine is to the effect that God does for us what we should do for ourselves, thus stunting our moral growth and keeping us immature. Everett in his *Moral Values* long ago pointed out that if the Christian doctrine of the atonement means fulfilling the law of right conduct for someone else it is at bottom immoral. Edgar Brightman used to stress how a false Christianity can rightly offend the morally sensitive, by pointing to theories of the atonement where God was supposed to fulfill the demands for man's right conduct, thus actually robbing man of his autonomy and preventing his becoming both right and morally mature. Christian atonement, obviously, cannot mean such a "substitution." Instead of reflecting damagingly on the wisdom and concern of

God Himself as Agape, Christian atonement illustrates these aspects of His nature; instead of by-passing the law, Christian atonement means its perfect fulfillment; instead of doing for men what they ought to do themselves to become real and right, God Himself enables men to do for themselves what is needed for their true righteousness and for their fullest possible moral maturity. What, then, can be a Christian conception of substitution? [5]

I. Substitution is Both Christian and Moral

Substitution, rather, is the essence of morality; it is substitution that makes morality social; whatever view of morality does not include substitution, at its center, is not Christian. The basic Hindu view of morality is in accordance with karma. In this doctrine each person is free to choose in relation to his relevant past and to be rewarded, immediately or in a deferred way, in accordance with his choice. Deed is followed by just consequence for each person. Morality at its heart, therefore, is not social. Social morality in Hinduism is a matter of *dharma,* or the social customs that facilitate the functioning of society. Ultimate morality for Hinduism is individualistic.

In the Christian view, on the contrary, there are individual

[5] It should be recognized how important are the studies of Vincent Taylor, who concludes that the New Testament doctrine, especially Paul's, declares God's act to be representative rather than substitutionary. But he himself maintains that God does something for us that we cannot do for ourselves. I believe this to be the noblest meaning of substitution. There can be substitution that involves the other fulfillingly. Any other understanding of substitution is immoral and unchristian.

responsibility and reward, but these are radically subordinate to social responsibility and reward. Deeper, too, than responsibility and reward lies the whole nature of morality that is not conceived of in terms of these factors. These enter in, to be sure, but not at the center. Therefore in order to understand the plain fact that substitution lies at the heart of Christian morality, and even goes beyond the realm of morality, we must examine the social nature of righteousness and salvation. After that we must inquire into the nature of sin as to whether or not that is similarly social.

Substitution, vicariousness, or representativeness, the acting in the place of, or in the stead of, another, underlies all knowledge, growth and grace. God, of course, is the fount of all knowledge, growth and grace. In the first place man has not made himself; he is a creature. Secondly, the fact that he can learn is a gift. The Spirit has breathed above the chaos, and out of nonbeing and confusion has brought life and harmony. Thirdly, knowledge, growth and grace have gradual beginnings in human history, and, indeed, in natural history. Men have discovered what they now know piecemeal, painfully, gradually and over the long ages. Each new generation is debtor to all that have gone before. Knowledge, growth and grace are part of a social history through which God has worked. The appropriation of each person and generation of the past is due to man's God-given capacity to recapitulate the history of the race in an amazing fashion.

As a matter of fact, the stark horror stares us in the face that knowledge, growth and grace have passed through an actual living on and off other lives to the point where nature exhibits this fact as a regular and intrinsic feature. The other side of this living on and off other lives is, of course, the sacrifice of life for other life as part and parcel of God's creation. The shedding of blood for others is part of the inner grain of the universe and cannot be by-passed on any level, certainly not in its deepest reaches of the complete self-giving of the *total* self, even the *total* life of God as *total* love unto death. Life in this sense is mostly substitute experience. It depends on vicariousness.

We live in the present, therefore, almost entirely because we appropriate the depths of life's tasks and meanings from the past. What we are, we are overwhelmingly because others have done something for us and in our stead. We ourselves do not now have to live through the whole process *de novo,* and we can be now what we are because others have done certain things and developed certain experiences vicariously. They have done them in our stead.

In the same way we are debtors to the present. Our own experience would be thin and shallow, in fact not even human, if it were not for parents and teachers who instruct us in the present. Books can also be communicators of contemporary experience. Our daily lives depend upon constant contacts with other human beings who stimulate what we are and know, who give us new contents and contexts of knowledge, who inspire us to growth and whose love is a means of grace. Man simply is not man apart from substitution. Vicariousness plays a major and indispensable role in all of human life. God comes mediated through man's history, and God's purpose becomes understood and partially expressed through our heritage, but He is also mediated by contemporary society. Growth thus comes representatively through present grace of knowledge. Knowledge comes by grace and work through a history of living. Both knowledge and growth, moreover, come from the original gift and working, the sustaining concern of God.

The more any creature becomes the object of the grace of God the more he bestows grace upon the world; the more he becomes the vicarious bringer of blessings. Such blessings, of course, involve new challenges, and can curse man apart from the right response to God's grace, but they come vicariously, doing for us what we ourselves do not have to do for the first time. The closer a person lives to God the more he makes a way for others to God.

What we have dealt with, however, are knowledge, growth and grace, not with morality. Can morality be social? Can we be *righteous* for anyone else? Let us be clear at this point. Knowledge, growth and grace all require human appropriation. They come to us beyond and before our own choosing and they come as a stream of power. They are not offered as neutral entities. They come working beyond the effort of any one person. They are social forces that surround and interpenetrate the very forms of thinking, knowing, choosing and growing. Yet apart from some personal understanding and consent their real purpose is not accomplished and their full power is not released. They cannot be dismissed without helping or hurting; and they cannot be treated as though they were not. They form part of the warp and woof of every person. No one can be isolated and live apart from his concrete social heritage and environment, but no person simply is his heritage or his environment. He responds. He chooses. He appropriates the past whether for fulfillment or frustration.

Thus morality is no neat, personal, rational choice apart from involvement in community. It receives its meaning and power of interpretation, dominant affections, depth response, and creative remaking in relation to community. Morality, therefore, at its depths, is social. It is substitutionary both from the past and from the present. We act as we do, and are able to act as we do, because others through the ages and in an innumerable company have acted and now act in our stead. Besides, Christian morality is also social in intent. To live the Christian life, the truth and the way, is to live for others, even as Christ lived for us and gave his life for us. The nature of mature morality is thus social at its very inception.

Christian morality is also social in standard. The Christian is not concerned with saving his life or with reward. He is concerned with the saving of others and with the coming of the Kingdom. His own life is expendable. His prayer is for grace to become more expendable. The Son of Man is He who gives His ransom for many and is also by this very token the Son of God. Jesus could not save his own life, his accusers riled, and rightly, as Harry Denman points out, for he who saves his own life cannot save the lives of others. In the Kingdom the last are the first; and the first, the last; the saints prefer one another in glory; and the laborers of an hour share fully with the laborers of a day. The Christian conception of morality in origin, aim and result is thus through and through social. Substitution, vicariousness, representativeness, doing for others that they might have a chance better than otherwise, doing *instead of others:* such is the inmost nature of true morality.

When we have said these things, we are not unmindful of our three objections to so-called atonement: the violation of the character of God Himself as *Agape,* the by-passing of the law, and the doing something for someone else that he ought to do for himself both in order to be righteous and to be mature. Nothing that we have written must be taken in such a sense as to violate any of these negative standards. As we come to develop the doctrine of the atonement we shall be under constant obligation to show at the end that all these requirements are satisfied. First, however, we must take up the second topic of inquiry: the social nature of sin.

Social sin seems a contradiction in terms. Is not sin the cutting off relations through faithlessness and rebellion? How, then, can sin be social? Let us look at a few possibilities.

In the Old Testament we find a clear illustration of one concept of social sin in the first few chapters of Leviticus. If a priest, the people, or any man sin unknowingly or unwittingly, when he finds out about his sin he shall offer the appropriate sacrifice unto the Lord. Sin is here considered a transgression of law. Whether or not a person or a people know about the law, its transgression constitutes sin. Thus a people can sin, as a people, when, as a people, they decide to do something that is contrary to the law, however subtle or self-deceived that decision may be, or when they do something contrary to a law that they do not know or have forgotten. Sin then is collective transgression. If sin is put on the level of mere law, whether in observance or in breach, there can, of course, be social sin. Sin is then a violation of objectively right relations.

Ezekiel, however, in the Old Testament saw sin as a category of personal responsibility. Guilt was a matter of personal action or culpable inaction. If a man warns the sinner, he is not guilty of his crime; if he does not warn him, however, he is guilty with him. Social sin is, then, an *acquiescence* in someone else's or in a people's sin, whether by participation or by not resisting it. The Letter of James in the New Testament has a similar definition: "Whoever knows what is right to do and fails to do it, for him it is sin" (4:17). Here we have a clearly personal responsibility for sin with no social reference. A deeper definition of sin, however, is Romans' "whatever does not proceed from faith is sin" (14:23). Neither passage, of course, must necessarily be interpreted individualistically (as in the case of Hindu karma), even though both passages are based on personal responsibility. Cannot people sin together whether through conscious transgression as through a root lack of faith?

In the New Testament, too, we have the theory that we have all sinned in Adam and may all live in Christ. Adam is the federal head of humanity who introduced sin. Since man cannot ever afterward escape bondage to sin, not being free to overcome it in himself, all must share in the dominion of sin. Such an understanding of sin is called "original sin." Inability to accept such a concept of sin is supposed nowadays to be a sign of theological shallowness. Naturally few modern theologians accept a literal Adam who lived a few thousand years ago. We are well beyond such ignorance now, and many Christian thinkers are almost up to honesty at this point. Therefore original sin in this specific historic sense is no longer tenable. Nevertheless, can we not keep an experiential doctrine of original sin, a social stream of sin into which we all enter by actual experience? The very nature of man [6] is to be so set on himself that from man's first sinning, whenever it was, no man has been able to rise above it, but rather, has been held fast in its clutches. Such a view of human nature, too, is not only individual but social in its intents and aspirations. Augustine held sin to be due to the inheritance of a defect of nature whereby man can no longer remain sinless. Can we not believe in a common human nature that has never been able to be sinless? Is not the original fact about man, from the very beginning of his humanity, the actuality of his being a sinner? If this

---

[6] Nature is here defined in its actual, not its potential state. *Eschatologically* human nature may be defined from the point of view of the perfection of Christ; *pedagogically* it must be seen as akin to the humiliation of Christ. We are discussing here the assumed rather than the consummated nature.

is a social fact, including all human beings, can we not say that sin is social? [7]

Can we not, however, dig a bit deeper than that? Is not sin man's way of cutting off his relations with God, whether through faithlessness or rebellion, or both? Do not sinners get together to build their own tower of Babel, their own sign and symbol of self-sufficiency? Does not man as an individual, too, participate in this social defense against God? Does not man know, deepest down below the explicit thought that he will not face, that he wants to be protected from the demands of God? Is not sin, then, far more than a merely personal revolt or lack of faith? Is it not the individual's joining, within his depth response, in man's enmity toward God and in helping to raise the idols that can take the place of God? Sin is social, then, as man's basic acceptance of the status quo. The acceptance of the stream of sin, man's actual half-truths and limited loyalties, may be a far deeper and qualitatively different sin from his own personal sinning. It is also far more insidious.

The state of sin in the self goes far below the acts of sin, of course; but does not man's total state of sin go qualitatively more deeply than any merely personal decisions and creations? Here man faces God as *total man, as man in his total involvement.* Can it be, then, that no amount of personal holiness or personal sinning can reach the depths and height of power that are embodied in social identification,

---

[7] For an excellent and suggestive study of the whole question of sin and atonement see Edward Ramsdell, *The Christian Perspective.*

whether of righteousness or of sin? Can this be the reason that people once preferred, and still do prefer, Barabbas to the Son of Man? Only in relation to original sin and original righteousness, man's deepest relation to God in either instance, does sin or righteousness become representative. Is this Messianic consciousness the identification with God at His deepest purpose for man to save him from the depths of original sin? Was Jesus' "being made sin" less a matter of his personal acts and decisions as such, than the way he entered into the whole heritage of human sin and with God's love and light challenged it to a fight to the finish?

We need to be careful, all the same, lest we make sin impersonal. No one can sin for anyone else. Sin is personal as well as social. Nor can anyone save anyone else. Grace is personal as well as social. In past writings I have refused to accept social sin or original sin because of this fact of genuine personal responsibility, a strong biblical category. I still want to keep this aspect of the stress. There are in each person a reality and a need to be respected that are inviolable. There is no sin or salvation *finally* that does not involve personal participation. There is, as a fact, a stream of sin that is filled by man's basic and continually reaffirmed revolt against God, his hiding from Him, or man's making his own half-gods. This process goes so deep into human history and human responses that it is passed off as worldly wisdom and as natural adjustment. Man, however, stands guilty as man because he acquiesces in the ways of the world which are enmity toward God.

If only man surrenders his life completely by faith and grace into the hands of God, he no longer wants to escape guilt. Then he craves no more to escape, but to warn the sinner of his guilt. His love binds him to his fellow man and he is willing with the Christ to "be made sin" for the world. In other words, whether as sinner or as saint, he belongs with man in his original sin. The stream of grace does not branch off into pleasant pastures and fragrant meadows, but runs the nearest way to the mud and muck of human sinfulness. Only by some such understanding of the social nature of morality and the social nature of sin shall we understand why the life and death of Jesus are no individual events but the center of our historic drama where Jesus loved and suffered *representatively* as both God and man. In this sense Jesus became "sin" in his voluntary acceptance of his people's burden of original sin.

Jesus himself inherited and appropriated substitute experience. He identified himself not only with the will of God but also with the good of man, and not only with man in general but also with his own people. Through the Dead Sea Scrolls we may come to understand more fully the silent period in Jesus' life. We may learn how he imbibed the best wisdom of the Essenes and beyond them identified himself with the great prophets. He may have come to consider himself the Teacher of Righteousness whom the Essenes expected. He may, furthermore, have identified his own life with the prophets both in their searing condemnation of evil and in their eager looking for a deliverer, God's chosen.

Wisdom literature, prophetic writings, apocalyptic hopes, and the Essenes' expectation of a Teacher of Righteousness may all have formed the deep background of that final breaking through of God the Son into human history through Christ, the fulfillment of time.

Jesus identified himself with increasing growth before both God and men with the fullest revelation of God in Israel, until open to the fullness of God, organically and conclusively, he expressed beyond the Old Israel at its height the New Israel at its universal level. Because Jesus recapitulated the history of God's revelation, by means of his acceptance at its conclusive level of man's best response to God, he became the supreme debtor to his people. His experience was uniquely the summary at the summit of human experience. It was peculiarly the maximum of substitute experience ever appropriated by man. Therefore his own experience all the way through, especially in its identification with our suffering, can become substitute experience and substitute righteousness for us.

For Jesus, Messianic identification with the Old Israel was an identification with the sufferings of his people. Whatever be the truth of the meaning for Jesus personally of the Suffering Servant of the Second Isaiah, in actuality Jesus so identified himself with his people's suffering that he became the Suffering Servant. The people found in him its suffering King. To suffer through love is to be like God and to be of God. The Kingship of Jesus was his becoming obedient unto death, suffering not by and for himself, but with and for his people. His suffering was more profound yet. Jesus identified himself, above all, with God, for he knew God to be love and he knew himself to be "the Son of His love." Such identification went all the way into the combat with man's original sin. Jesus entered the deep, dark places of man's hiding from God. He tore the veil from men's eyes and made them see their religious pretensions and falsifications. People's hatred of Jesus was therefore their hatred of God.

Jesus was condemned in fact because he made himself God.[8] He acted as God in human history because he knew God acted in him. The Father and he were One in the holy Love who by His light of life condemned sin in the flesh. The Father and he were One in their redemptive suffering and power to redeem from sin. The Father and he were One in their power to forgive sin and to make others become the Sons of God. On the other hand, Jesus had identified himself with his people and with generic man in such a way that his people and generic man stood under the same condemnation. Jesus then assumed their guilt, accepted their suffering, and offered them the eternal victory of his union with God. In Jesus we have history's climax of substitutionary, vicari-

---

[8] Tillich's assertion that Jesus became transparent to God by refusing to make anything finite infinite (*The Dynamics of Faith*) has to contend with the accusation against Jesus that he, a human being, made himself God. We have to understand and to select the right picture of Jesus if Tillich's approach is to stand. The fact seems to be that he both refused to do so (no one is good but God) and also did so (I and the Father are one). Both sides can be reconciled, however, if he knew that the reality and power in him was God, so that it was the Father who did the mighty works and told him what to announce. Then he both denied and affirmed that he was God, as was right for him to do.

ous, or representative experience, both of suffering and of victory, both in the Cross and in the Resurrection. Such substitution lies at the base of all human experience and measures our reality and salvation. The kind of vicariousness actually appropriated by us determines the kind of our existence. Our basic decision in life is whether we are to appropriate the stream of original sin, justifying ourselves by means of it, perhaps largely in terms of religious or idealistic camouflages, or whether we are willing to take up the Cross of redemptive suffering, becoming God's means to channel into human history His saving grace.

Man's basic choice is always between these two streams, between God and demonic depths of evil. Man is not free to live independent of these cosmically antagonistic forces. He may not suspend judgment or find neutral ground. He is for or against Christ, for or against God in human history. The cosmic and historic significance of the atonement comes to light only in view of such reality of a dramatic dualism of history and of the necessity and decisive function of representative experience. Without an understanding of substitutionary, vicarious or representative atonement, we shall fail to be realistic and right about the finality of the Christian revelation that centers in the atonement.

II. Why Jesus Died for Us

Did Jesus have to die for us? This question is often asked. Let us now look at it in the light of the preceding discussion.

The sinner as sinner rejects love. His worst dread is love,

for love threatens the nature of his security that is built around fear of some kind. Faithlessness and rebellion against God make for a depth dimension of fear that drives man to erect protection against God. The biggest job fearful man has to do is to deceive himself. He can never deceive his deepest self, however, and is, therefore, constantly vulnerable and never secure. He camouflages his hatred toward God and his fear of Him, in its ultimate power, behind a substitute religion. Such religion often becomes very high and beautiful, but always helps to forestall his total surrender to Love.

Fear and Love can never co-exist peaceably. They are battlers always, and to death. No boundary line can be drawn between them and no concordat of convenience. The war may seem sham and peace may even be the surface appearance. All the same, the war rages between sinner and God, between fear and Love. The more unqualified Love is, the more severely it judges and the more it becomes hated. When Jesus as Agape Himself comes, sin is judged in its ultimate dimension, because God as Love has come. The more novel the Love is, too, the more readily it is rejected because the sinner has had little time to dilute or distort his understanding of it. The sinner is caught unprepared and defenseless. He is surprised from behind and the dreaded Love enters into the courtyard of his life before he has had a chance to ward it off.

The sinner can hide from God no matter how God comes, because man's true freedom provides him inviolable integrity.

God never forces Himself on the sinner. Love never comes in such a manner. When God has been shut out in one way, however, He comes in another. In His fullness He came in One who unexpectedly took the religious tradition of his people, its noblest sayings and aspirations, and filled them full to overflowing and to radical remaking by the presence of God as Agape. The sinner, saint and secular alike, stood then without protection from the white heat of full Love. God broke into the world with the Radical Love He is, and shocked that world into maddened fury.

Hate and fear could not give in. The sinners were not ready to capitulate. Particularly terrible was the fate of the religious leaders who stood exposed in ugly nakedness. The half-gods became not glorious, but ugly idols, in the light of the true God. Their most devoted worshipers became destructive and dangerous to the God of universal Love. The higher the devotion the madder the fury. It is high religion that suffers the most when the Most High draws near. Therefore there was no chance at all for the world of original sin to welcome outright the Savior. When God's saving Love came as the Son himself, he had to be rejected and done away. The stream of original sin was not to be stopped and turned into the river of grace. It beat against the most dreaded of all obstacles. The Son of Man who was also the Son of God's Love had to be removed. The simple answer to our question: "Did Jesus have to die?" from the point of view of sin is that sinners could not but kill the Son of Man for he was also the Son of God.

On the other side, the stream of grace had become full and neither could it be turned. The fullness of time had come with the fullness of God. Because Jesus had in his life, as its dominant reality, the presence of God Himself as holy Love, Jesus could not turn away from Calvary. We are not saying, of course, that Jesus was not free and that logically and humanly he could not have run away before, or in, Gethsemane. We are saying, rather, that actually Jesus' eros had been so penetrated and molded by Agape that no such choice was fully real for him.[9] He had set his face to go to Jerusalem. He had counted the cost. He had paid the price. God Incarnate cannot do less than identify Himself completely with sinful man and for sinful man face death. Jesus had committed the crime unpardonable by man: the removing of man's insulation from God. Jesus had made God real to the people and had let Him draw near to man. No worse "crime" can be committed by any human being! But precisely because Jesus, representing in this life God Himself, had opened man's eyes to the full truth of God, giving them no excuse for their sins, he himself could not acquiesce in that sin and must therefore become its victor. Thus from the point of view of God as well as that of man, Jesus had to die for man's sin.

[9] In this sense of victory over eros Jesus could be sinless and still know sin. He could know anxiety, having felt its craving, claim, and real power, even its horrible burden, without ever giving way to it, continually receiving power to bear anxiety without ever deliberately accepting it. Even though such a view of sin may be too rationalistic, moralistic and shallow, nevertheless in some such way, I believe, come together God's assuming sin in Jesus and Jesus' victory over it.

The struggle had first been to death within Jesus. He himself as a human being had lost his life in God to find it a new creature. He had himself, as a human being, been at some final point born again from the stage of temptation and alienation, from the dominion of sin into the glorious liberty of the Son of God. Sin with him may not have been so much personal as representative. He was born into a world of original sin. From below this was his heritage of substitutionary experience. In love he identified himself with man and by nature he bore the brunt of sin's sting. But his conclusive orientation was to God and his dominant identification was with the eternal Son. By the power of the Spirit and of the Father's teaching and working in him, he proved what it is to be human at the level of original sin, even as he "was made sin" for us. God Himself identified Himself in and with this man, in and with guilty man, empowering the true man, the man of grace, the man of God, in such a way that sin became canceled from within, law fulfilled from within, and death conquered from within. Man without God was forever the prisoner and slave of law, sin and death. Emmanuel made a lasting victory over man's enemies both in principle and in fact.

The struggle was to death not only within Jesus, but also at the center of history itself.[10] Here the stream of man's

[10] Cf. Elias of Crete: "The saint applies the name of *drama* to that which our Saviour endured as representing mankind. He does not mean that it was unreal and fictitious, like other dramas, but only that Christ impersonates and plays the part of the human race" (as cited in J. E. L. Oulton, *The Mystery of the Cross*, p. 24).

original sin met the stream of God's endless grace head on. Since God was the chief actor the victory was eternal; since the whole nature of the cosmos, the very purpose of creation, was involved, the victory was cosmic; since history itself here came to its midpoint, the victory was historic. For the struggle meant victory. God never loses. Love never fails. The fullness of time means the fullness of victory. Its results may have to be worked out in freedom over unimaginable stretches of time. God's sovereign initiative needs man's willing response. But victory had to be. No lesser outcome was possible.

The struggle and victory were both objective and subjective. What happened objectively on Calvary? Why did time become full when atonement fulfilled creation and revelation? From eternity God's love and holiness now made a way in history for their functional harmonization. Holiness, in one of its aspects, is God's complete rejection of sin in the sinner for the sake of the sinner. It is His own perfect purity that He longs to bestow on the sinner and cannot until the sinner wants to have it. Holiness is God's holding off the sinner both from Himself and from the sinner's true satisfactions in order that the sinner may come both to God, his true home, and to his own true self, his destined end. Love, on the other hand, is God's unconditional search for the sinner. It is God's wanting him near in companionship. It is God's own self-giving for the sinner that He may draw him unto Himself and have him with Himself. Holiness and love must therefore work in opposite directions, even when they are workings of the same God. There is pain in God's heart because He both wants the sinner near Him and yet, for the sinner's sake and in line with God's own purity, He must hold the sinner off from Himself. Calvary is the means by which God makes clear, powerful and open the way of salvation for man whereby the functional tension at the very heart of God, because of man's sin, is capable of being removed.

Similarly man is in contradiction. He wants the love of God but not His holiness. Man feels at the depths of his being that in God love and holiness cannot be separated for God is holy Love. Therefore man lives ambivalently. He both flees from God in dread and searches for Him, as though God were not offering Himself to man! Before Calvary—the complete self-giving of Agape unto death— the contradiction in man never reached its maximum. With the death of Jesus sin became illumined and judged at its lowest depths. At the same time the love of God was declared at its highest heights. The more the Gospel is truly preached and actually reaches man the more also man is put in conflict at the center of his being. He is caught in the cosmic struggle between original sin and redemptive grace, between demonic evil at its basest and God at His most gracious invitation.

Calvary, as we shall see in our third section, is the place and power for the resolution of the tension in God and the contradiction in man. Calvary, therefore, relates to what is eternal, cosmic, historic and human. It is fully objective and fully subjective. Atonement is realism at the center of Reality and of life.

The struggle between God in Christ and original sin was a struggle to death whatever form the conflict took. We know that Jesus died on the Cross and that therefore the Cross marks the fullness of time. We have no right to speculate about history. Rather than speculate, we receive or reject what God has done. At the same time we have no right to limit the power and wisdom of God to His historic revelation. For one thing, God has unending possibilities at hand even while He uses some rather than others. For another thing, history is revelation in terms of both God's acts and man's response. The history of Incarnation is incomparably the work of God by His personal coming into human life, but it is also our reception and interpretation of His coming.

The Cross, in other words, as the *form* of God's suffering is conditioned by its happening in the Roman Empire. On the Cross God went all the way to death with and for man. The Cross still comes to man, and often all the way to death, but the suffering is in concentration camps, in modern forms of liquidation and in the long mental tortures of those who follow the Christ in fact inflicted by those who hide behind their confession of him while denying him both in their theologies and in their spirit. The only criterion of the Cross is God's full presence with man, suffering until the cup overflows the brim of life. Therefore the Cross of Jesus is both the summary of man's actual suffering in One whose life means Emmanuel, God with us; and also the symbol of all future redemptive suffering on the part of those who, in identification with man's sin, sorrow and suffering, will know the reality of Agape.

The struggle thus neither began nor ended with Calvary. The Cross starts eternally in the heart of God. The Lamb is slain before the foundation of the world and the way of the Cross is as old as the creative Love of God. Its earthly actualization is no accident of time; its concrete form of realization, of course, is contingent. The Cross is also prefigured by the paschal lamb and postfigured by the eucharistic sacrifice. The paschal lamb is the symbol and the rite of Love's suffering anywhere on any level less than Agape, for where Love is, there is God. The paschal lamb exhibits the preparatory suffering of God in man on a subagapaic level. The eucharistic sacrifice, on the other hand, stands for the sacrifice of Love understood and accepted. God's universal, victorious Love is the only standard for the Source in Reality of redemptive suffering. Calvary gathers up all the redemptive suffering of the past and is the divine invitation and power for the future. Christ is truly history in the human Jesus. In him God suffered in and with man. But He came as the Preparer, with creation and with the dawn of human history; and He is with us personally unto the end of the world.

Wherever Love is, there is the Christ, atoning in some form, however, undeveloped. The only begotten Son, who came as the fullness of time in Jesus, Himself prepared for the fullness of time in countless others; and must keep suffering in us until for the sake of the universal Church there is completed in the body of disciples what is lacking in the Christ's afflictions (Col. 1:24). The fact that the atonement is thus inclusive both in the cosmic and the historic sense, demonstrating the heart of God and the center of history, in no way detracts from its decisive work and manifestation in Jesus as the Christ. We turn, therefore, to our third point. The universality of God's presence in redemptive human suffering, defined and definitely enacted in Jesus, is precisely what declares Jesus, on the level of redemption, to be the Christ of God.

III.   THE MEANING OF CALVARY

What, then, happened on Calvary? What is the concrete meaning and power of the redemptive Christ-deed? There are three answers, each fulfilling the other. Again, we repeat, each of the following answers presupposes the answers yet to follow. Even so, when we have given them all we stand amazed at our shallowness in comparison to reality and aghast at our poverty of words in comparison even to one life-shaking experience of God's grace. We agree readily with Jean Nicolas Grou who said: "Here we have matter of contemplation for all eternity, and all that we shall think of it and all that we shall say of it in heaven, will be infinitely less than the truth." [11] We must speak in this way because we are human beings who at our best speak in human words. Only as the Spirit speaks the spiritual truth through

[11] *How to Pray,* p. 31.

and beyond our lines and lives shall the truth itself have any adequate say.

In the first place, Jesus died as our example. We could call this the lowest form of the interpretation of the atonement. We shall not do so, for nothing that God does, or provides for, ought to be called "low." Let us, rather, say that such a doctrine is true, albeit there are more adequate answers.

Jesus died for us as an example in at least four ways. He is our example of obedience. He is the pioneer of our faith because he became obedient unto death, yes, the death of the Cross. Even as he surrendered his every hope and plan unto God and set his face steadfastly toward Jerusalem, even so must we surrender our lives unto God every whit. There can be no salvation at all for us until we learn to take up our cross to follow the Christ.

Jesus was also an example of faith. Having been heard because of his obedience and his trust in God, the Father above Jesus and the Son within Jesus made it possible for us, as we trust in the Agape God, to have our hearts cleansed by faith. Gethsemane and Calvary are climactic illustrations of what faith can do when man is willing to become obedient unto death. Faith is not merely some belief about God. Faith is mostly the presence of God in our lives. God can so interpenetrate our spirits that even when God the Father cannot be encountered and we cry in our loneliness, "My God, my God, why hast thou forsaken me," we find the longer answer, after our spirits penetrated with the divine Spirit have drained the cup, "Father, unto thy hands I commit my spirit." Such obedience and such faith help our accepting "so great a salvation."

Jesus also became the example of humility. The mind of Christ for us means the mind that seeks not its own, prefers others in honor, ministers to those in need without regard to status, makes itself of no reputation and becomes simple as a child. Because Jesus was willing to make himself of no reputation and become obedient unto death God has given him a name above all others. The name of Jesus is highest precisely because he never was concerned about his own name. Later disciples make external honor to his name the criterion of being saved and thus crucify him afresh. Jesus is Lord in the sense that he is the incarnation in the fullness of time of God who is Agape. He is Lord only through his identification with God who is Agape. The craving for external honor, authority and glory for him or in his name is surely an abomination both to God and to His Son.

God became Emmanuel in Jesus because Jesus understood and accepted the God who seeks no glory but whose glory is to bestow glory. Those who, like Jesus, make themselves of no reputation and become obedient unto death, in their deepest decision before God, can fathom the meaning of Jesus as the example of our humility: he enmanned God Himself. Not until God's presence in us burns out self-seeking and glory-seeking can we understand and accept the atonement by grace and faith.

Above all, however, Jesus is the example of love. The only adequate example of love is Love. God is Love and we never know, let alone receive God, until we know and receive Love. The Bible instructs us to be imitators of God and specifies that such imitation involves our walking in love, the kind of Love who Jesus was and demonstrated by giving himself for us (Eph. 5:1-2). To walk in the reality of atonement means to accept the full forgiveness of God's love, an act that also involves our own self-forgiveness and self-acceptance. To walk in the Spirit means to walk in the way of Love, for God is Love. Love is the fulfillment of the law. God alone can fulfill the law in us. We must accept the righteousness of Christ. Our own righteousness will never cover us. Yet that righteousness is precisely Agape.

Possibly we might view the example of Jesus, then, not as the fullness of atonement but as the content of life, the fruit of the Spirit, that is the criterion of the reality of atonement. Atonement involves our walking even as Jesus walked in obedience, faith, humility and love. Unless we become ambassadors of the living Christ by grace and faith to the degree that the dominant drive of our lives is to have men reconciled with God and therefore with one another, we have never tasted the reality of atonement. To be atoned involves our receiving the heart of Christ, the eyes of faith and the fruit of the Spirit. Those who know the reality of atonement are constrained to focus their lives on the coming of the Kingdom where Love is Lord. Their new hearts are in heaven, being with Christ, but also on earth, for in them Christ comes down in their own day to make whole, to remove the veil of ignorance, and to break down the partitions of fear, envy, hate and greed. Atonement demands that those who accept God's Christ-deed for them join the Christ in his conflict unto death, and unto the end of human time, against original sin. That Jesus becomes our example of love means that we identify ourselves with him both in his identification with the Father and in his redemptive struggle, suffering, death and victory, against all that keeps men locked in themselves and barred away from one another. Atonement then matters essentially, operationally, to actual life, individual and social. Unless men as individuals and communities change in line with the example of Jesus there is no real atonement. Jesus is thus, in the first place, our example. Atonement can mean *nothing less* than this. It must mean *much more!*

The atonement, then, is never understood on the Christian level if it stops with any "moral influence" theory. God was in Christ reconciling the world to Himself, but not chiefly by giving us a light and a way. He gave us light by Life; He gave us also *the power to walk in the way.* Jesus lived and died to give us power for salvation. By accepting the fullness of the Love of God from Him who eternally is God, there came to be a union of God and man whereby a whole new stream of redemption was opened for man. This stream first came out of eternity; in history ever since the beginning of humanity the stream of grace had been making its hard and costly way against the stream of original sin. On Calvary the flood of grace broke through and became fully and openly available for man. One of the greatest of all Christian hymns well expresses this fact:

> There is a fountain filled with blood
> Drawn from Emmanuel's veins;
> And sinners, plunged beneath its flood,
> Lose all their guilty stains.

God did in Jesus Christ what man could never do for himself or by himself. God made in Christ a living way "through his flesh" (Heb. 10:20).[12] God being the constitutive reality of the Godman the flesh and blood of Jesus were the flesh and blood of God.[13] It was God—as well as man—who went to the Cross. It was God who carried our sins on the tree. It was God who set us forever and fully free. We do not deny or diminish one whit the human nature of Jesus, but the human was willingly joined to, controlled

[12] We mean by "flesh," of course, the biblical wholeness of man. Cf. G. L. Prestige, *Fathers and Heretics,* p. 105: "By 'flesh' the Bible repeatedly designates human nature in its fullness, and the Fathers followed the same usage."

[13] Cf. Irenaeus, *Against Heresies,* in Richardson, *op. cit.,* p. 382: "Those who separate Jesus from Christ and say Christ remained impassible while Jesus suffered, and try to bring forward the Gospel According to Mark, can be corrected out of that, if they will read it with a love of the truth." I hold that God suffered in and with Jesus because He is redemptive Love. Obviously as God He did not suffer as man suffers. The anxiety of the dying Jesus, his estrangement, his doubt were not God's. But the very constitutive Godhood of Jesus' personality that made the Cross necessary and that accepted the Cross within and with the human, actually suffered for us. Such is the wonder and glory of redemptive Love. God's suffering is because of the perfection of His identification with us, not because of

by, and expressive of, the divine. To miss the point of God's own complete self-giving for us is to miss the meaning of the atonement. The atonement was and is through and through the work of Agape. There can therefore be no salvation outside the blood of God, His complete self-giving for us unto death and His conquering of death, sin and law from within our humanity.

A sideline interpretation of the blood of Christ may enlarge this conception of the body and blood of God. The blood runs in the body. The body of Christ is now the Church. The blood of God's complete self-giving for us that once ran actually on Calvary now keeps flowing in the Church. The Church is the community of God's complete self-giving for the world. Those who accept God as Agape, in actual intention and by grace, are in fact the Church. The Church consists of all who live "Christ and him crucified." The Church is the fellowship of the dead-to-themselves and the alive-for-Christ. They no longer live but Christ lives

lack of perfect power which is the human characteristic in such suffering. Therefore we cannot agree with Cyril of Alexandria when he writes: "And we confess that he who was begotten from God the Father as Son and God only-begotten, though being by his own nature impassible, suffered in the flesh for us, according to the Scriptures, and he was in the crucified flesh impassibly making his own the sufferings of his own flesh" (Hardy, *Christology of the Late Fathers,* p. 351). Possibly Cyril's *intention,* freed from Greek philosophical presuppositions, can be guarded in modern terms. (Cf. my *Evil and the Christian Faith,* chap. IX, "God and Suffering.") We should remember that the philosophy of substance also underlay the Formula of Union of 433. "In addition we all confess that the Word of God is impassible, though in his all-wise dispensation of the mystery, he is seen to attribute to himself the sufferings undergone by his own flesh. So the all-wise Peter spoke of Christ suffering for us in the flesh, and not in the nature of the ineffable Godhead" (Hardy, *op. cit.,* pp. 357-58).

in them a resurrection life. In this body of Christ runs the blood of God for the world. The blood is nothing but the very life of God's love. What the blood of God really means is the purity, grace, strength and suffering of God, wherein alone we can be saved.

The function of the blood is to nourish, to cleanse, to heal, and to keep in balance. Mankind is soul-sick with sin. We must all be healed. Apart from our coming "under the blood" of Christ there can be no healing. Only as we accept God's suffering for us and His forgiveness of us because He has made and makes a new righteousness for us in Christ, can we be saved. Not until we join the inclusive and wholly redemptive fellowship in Christ through grace and faith can we know the power of salvation. The power is in the blood, for life is in the blood, and the life of God for sin is in the blood of God. The power for universal love and community, that is, comes only within the right relationship to God, God's own open and free life flowing in us and through us. To be healed we must forsake our wretched self-seeking, our striving to be saved, and trust God who has Himself come, and who Himself comes, to save us by His blood.

Another function of the blood is to cleanse. Once healed, we must be cleansed over and over again. As the blood-stream flows into our lives and covers us wholly we are cleansed of our sins and made pure by the blood. The holiness of God has come basically with our being *healed* by the blood, but the holiness of God in us is ever in need of renewal. No one can remain holy except by the power of the blood. Only as God's purity overflows our total selves and removes every stain of life can we remain in Him apart from whom there is no salvation. When we come to understand what the blood really means we sing its reality. God Himself has come, and comes, to suffer and die for us that we might be made clean and stay clean. He waits and woos to give us His own shining holiness even as we become partakers of His life in His body. The purity of Christ comes through the power of God's self-giving Love which is the actual shedding of His blood for us, the total running out of him of His own life; for such total self-giving of God is the total victory of God over all that defiles. The body of mankind is, so to speak, diseased by sin. Original sin certainly is a disease! Jesus "caught" the disease but God's health was in him to overcome it. He developed the antibodies needed for our cure. As we accept these antibodies, God's power to cure the world's disease of sin, we receive the power to be healed.

The blood also nourishes. We need to be fed on the Word of God. We need intellectual feeding, to be sure, but, more, we need the feeding of our spirits on the blood and body of Christ. Such feeding is no external act. It is entering within the universal community of Christ's love and sharing his life. The sacraments are more than symbols. They are actual means of grace. The Word should be more than preached, it should also be acted. Preached, it reaches the mind through meaning. Acted, it reaches the spirit through Spirit. The preached Word presupposes the acted Word; the teaching of God's self-giving, the act of God's self-giving. Preaching is full only in relation to sacramental worship in the deepest sense of that word. We "feed on Christ" when we let his self-giving become our self-giving. We as branches find nourishment in the Vine. Thus as we receive God's gracious sacrifice in faith, our own lives are nourished unto everlasting life, now and in the life to come. Thus the blood shed and the body broken are actually the means of our living as sons of God. God gives us the power through the blood to keep on being His children and to grow even as we are healed, cleansed and nourished by the blood of the living Christ who, dying, released the flow of redemptive grace in human history and made a living way to God.

The blood also preserves the balance of the body. The process of interaction between metabolism and katabolism is dependent on the bloodstream. The blood carries the enzymes that keep harmony and balance in the life of the body. In the community of God is creative balance. God's love creates, maintains, and restores harmony to fellowship. Life is kept in order as we live within the bloodstream of God's love poured out for the world. No materialistic literalism of blood, but the true signification of blood needs to be understood. We are saved by the blood as God's own suffering and victorious identification with the world, conclusively in Jesus' Cross and Resurrection, and continuously insofar as the Church, by that Cross—God's conclusive self-giving for the world—takes up its cross of God's concern for the world, and experiences within that suffering, the victorious power of God's victory over evil, the Resurrection.

Need we point out that even as the human Jesus became the vehicle of the redemptive love of God, even so our humanity must participate in the reality and work of Christ? We must become co-workers with God in redemption, not in the sense that our humanity can achieve any way to God, but in the sense that our humanity becomes the means whereby God finds a way to man. The pump runs not without priming. Even as the blood of Jesus opened up a whole new era of redemption, even so we must participate in its continuing history. We must offer our lives to be crucified with the Savior. As Luther declares, we must become saviors to others. We never know Christ as Savior until the eternal Son of God dies in us to and for the world, and until we live and die unto Him for the world.

The conclusive act of power has been performed in Jesus. The way has been opened once for all. The power has come. Yet the way is the way of love and the power is the power of the Son of God's love. Such a way and such a power are continued only in the manner in which he once came. It is continued in the church not as a shrine or as a depository, but as the continuing humanity of Jesus, as the perpetuating human nature of the Son of God, wherein and whereby there is an ever-continued demonstration to the world of the reality of God as Redeemer. We join the church when we join the stream of redemption. We join the church when our hearts are moved by the living Christ, the eternal Son, to let him

rule our lives, which is precisely to be given in complete
dedication and service to the world. Christ in us is now and
ever the hope of glory, for the Christ who came must keep
coming through his body, the holy redemptive community
called the Church. We repeat, therefore Bultmann's crucial
sentence: "By giving us Jesus to be crucified, God has set up
the Cross for us." [14] Torrance has expressed this truth memor-
ably: "The Church is, so to speak, the atonement becoming
actual among men in the resurrection of a new humanity." [15]

Jesus died, then, as our example of obedience, faith, humility and love. He died also as our enabler to become Sons
of God. Fulfilling these two, however, he died as the perfect
sacrifice for our sins.

Sacrifice can be looked at wrongly and rightly. The wrong
way to see it is as placating the wrath of God. God, in such
a view, would need some prestation, some offering, to change
not only His mind but His heart. Such a view of sacrifice
borders on black magic and at its best presupposes an unworthy view of God. Neither does God need to satisfy any
devil. God, rather, does the sacrificing for us. That is the
right view of sacrifice. The eternal Father comes Himself
as the Son, the eternally outgoing Love of God, to participate
in man's desperate plight and to make a way out of it. God
gives Himself, suffers Himself, is Himself conversant with
man's sin, suffering and sorrow *from within man* in order
that by His deathless strength He might conquer death,

---

[14] "New Testament and Mythology," in Bartsch, *Kerygma and Myth*, p. 36.
[15] "The Atonement and the Oneness of the Church," in *Scottish Journal of Theology*, Vol. 7, no. 3, Sept., 1954, p. 268.

that by His unquenchable joy He might relieve man's sorrow, that by His sinless purity He might forever vanquish sin. Because God Himself is in man, man, in right relation to God and through the power of God, can do what man apart from such personal presence of God cannot do. God acts in man's stead, but by a substitution that involves man's responsible and willing participation as a consequence. He sacrifices Himself for man in order that by His stripes we may be healed. He who is deathless goes all the way to death in order that death might die.[16] He who is sinless becomes sin that sin might be slain. He who is unutterable joy becomes the Man of Sorrows that sorrow might be broken in His body.

Incarnation is the key to all ultimate truth for humanity. Man is made for God, but not until God becomes man can man become man. There was no other good enough to pay the price of sin. Only God can achieve perfect holiness;

[16] In this instance I agree with Athanasius that although Jesus had died, nevertheless since he was the Word, he could not taste death as God. God as Agape went all the way to the death of the Cross, sharing the suffering, giving the divine strength to the ego of Jesus, insofar as the human appropriated it. Thus the Incarnate Son of God went to death for us without God's dying. The deathless Love died out of the ego-consciousness of Jesus that ceased in death, but the deathless Son of God, the eternal Word, remained deathless to resurrect Jesus. Thus it is right to say both that God raised Jesus, as the New Testament usually does, and to say that the Son raised himself, since the constitutive reality of the Son never died. The union was temporarily dissolved by death, even as our union with God will be dissolved until we participate in Him again after our own resurrection from the dead. Therefore Athanasius can say that Christ raised his own body from the dead, without being docetic in doctrine. Cf. Hardy, *op. cit.,* p. 86. Apollinaris, however, not believing in the full humanity of Jesus, had to hold that "his Godhead also was put to death with his body, and thus was raised again from the dead by the Father" (*ibid.,* p. 231).

only He can bestow perfect holiness through His own sacrifice. God alone is good enough and strong enough to restore what the locusts have eaten. When the relation between man and God is broken, God alone can repair it. But such work of redemption is no external work. It is in, through and with man, as well as for man. The whole secret of the Incarnation and of incarnational theology is exactly that God becomes man in order that in God and by God we be saved, yet saved not externally, but from within our own true nature, or from our nature fulfilled by God's presence, purpose and power. Forgiveness and acceptance by God, of God and through God of all men is the only way to self-fulfillment and to the fulfillment of community. Is it any wonder that Bishop Aulén calls the emphasis on *God's* coming, *God's* paying, *God's* suffering, "the classical motif" of the atonement?

At the end, however, we must return to the fact that God becomes man, entering organically into the fulfilling relation to our humanity, in order that we might in that way be more truly ourselves as well. Calvary exhibits God's complete self-giving for man, but it also exhibits man's conclusive self-giving to God. In a way it is equally wrong to say either that God suffered for man or that man suffered in obedience and love for God, for on Calvary God and man cannot thus be separated. Our doctrine is not that of two Sons, nor of God *and* of man, but rather of the Godman. Only by keeping man real as man and doing for and in himself what is right can we have a moral theory of atonement. The whole stress, therefore, must be on *Incarnation,* the innermost secret of all creation, revelation and redemption: *God in man.* Redemption depends on Incarnation, *God in man,* and alone raises creation and revelation to the full understanding of the God who is Agape and demonstrates that fact once for all on Calvary. Incarnation as the full reality of God and man organically related through both God's nature of Agape and man's nature as the creation by and for Agape can alone give reason for the full hope of our Christian faith. God came *to* man, identifying Himself with man, because He loved him; God came *in* man, thus being even more intimately one with him, because He respected him. Well did Augustine stress the double character of the atonement as the work of both God and man: "the same person is at once God and man: God our goal, man our road." [17]

We have seen, then, the critical case of redemption. Unless we have an adequate understanding of the atonement as the actualization of the Love of God in human history we shall never reach an adequate Christian theology. Christian theology presupposes atonement by its very view of human freedom and of human nature. Creation, revelation and history come to a focus on Calvary where God goes to death for man, but in and with man, that man might willingly and lovingly come to know the Creator who is also Father and Friend.

It is also well to recall that atonement is a means, not an end. The end is Resurrection. The end is never redemptive

[17] *De civitate dei,* 11. 2.

suffering, but the community of the redeemed. The end is never the Cross as Cross, but the communion of saints. The end is never the pedagogical process or the redemptive process, but the eternal purpose to reveal through the church triumphant the manifold mysteries of God. Not the juridical perspective, not the legal dimension, but the perspective of love's fellowship and the dimension of the community of the understood and accepted grace of God are the final considerations of the Christian faith.

In the Letter to the Hebrews it is written that the mercy seat was overshadowed by the seraphim of glory. So be it at last and forever! The glory of God is the end for which the mercy seat was built. That glory, however, no theology can pen. There are dramatic symbols that go below language: of art, literature and music. There are dimensions of experience below thought, even below the inner articulation of our own experience. There are depths of God's reality below all human understanding. The Love of God surpasses *all* knowledge. Perhaps some Hallelujah Chorus can occasionally break through our torpor; perhaps some statue of Christ can capture depths of reality below our ordinary apprehension; perhaps some passage of literature might lay hold on the self called out by God, far in front of any present actualization. In the end, however, no experience and no interpretation can more than hint at the reality and the ways of His Love who suffered for us on Calvary and made for us once for all a living way to full forgiveness and newness of life.

IV

CHRIST AND THE CHRISTIAN

ONE large section of problems in Christology has to do with
the relation of Jesus to us. There is a strong desire, even
demand, that Jesus, in order to be the Son of God, must
be unique. Somehow Incarnation itself seems imperiled if
the Spirit who was in Jesus can be in us also. This fact must
be faced. A treatment of three topics: God and Jesus, God
and humanity, and the uniqueness of Jesus, should throw
light on this question. If these topics are adequately handled,
the relation between Christ and the Christian ought thereby
to be clarified.

I. THE RELATION OF JESUS TO GOD

If we resolutely start with Christ as Agape, what is the
relation of Jesus to God? [1] Traditionally, the eternal Son
of God became incarnate either *as* or *in* the historic Jesus.

---

[1] This is the basic question. Von Speyer is right: "The answer to every
question in the world lies hidden in the Father. There is no question
which was not first of all an answer. All questions come from the answer
and return to the answer" (*The Word,* p. 144).

According to the former of these two views Jesus is merely the historic name for the Second Person of the Trinity. The humanity is merely the guise and the means for the Son's historic appearance and work. There is only one ego, that of the eternal Son. Therefore the name Jesus can legitimately be applied to the Son before the Incarnation.[2] Jesus' real relation to God is, consequently, eternally as the second Person of the Trinity, who did descend to earth in human form and in human time to reveal God and to work out our salvation.

According to the latter view, God incarnate *in* the historic Jesus, God as Son became incarnate in a real human being.[3] The pre-existent Son is God's eternally outgoing Love who became conclusively declared and essentially effective in Jesus as the Christ. Jesus cannot therefore be the proper designation of the eternal Son, only of the incarnate Son. Jesus, accordingly, is constitutively related to God as both God and man. We cannot speak legitimately of Jesus' *becoming* incarnate, for Jesus is the historic person who became both the object and the subject of the Incarnation. God came in him and was received by him. Nor can we speak of Jesus after the Incarnation as simply the eternal Son of God. To do so would be to deny the reality of the Incarnation,

[2] As a matter of historic fact, I believe, the Fathers understood the name Jesus to refer to the incarnate Son, while it is now usual to hear such expressions as "Jesus came down from heaven," or "Jesus came to save us."

[3] Leo was surely right in claiming that "it was equally dangerous to believe the Lord Jesus Christ to be merely God and not man or merely man and not God" (Hardy, *Christology of the Late Fathers*, p. 366).

to dissolve the incarnate Son of God. The hypostatic union was real and permanent. To call Jesus the eternal Son after the Incarnation would be either to separate the two natures or to deny the permanent nature of Jesus' humanity.

The view that God became incarnate *as* the historic Jesus usually holds that God is one in nature but exists in three distinct personalities: [4] The Father never becomes incarnate; [5] the Son did, in the fullness of time; when He returned to heaven, He sent back to earth the third Person, the Holy Spirit. When the Son returned to heaven, He shed His human guise and all things were then essentially as before He left. Such is a rather common form of trinitarianism. A few, of course, hold that Jesus is the only God there is, was in heaven before He came to earth, and returned once again as the Holy Spirit. This position, however, is mostly unreflective and modern, whereas the tri-theistic trinitarian form has ancient lineage and sober scholarship behind it.[6] Actually this view, as we have intimated, is tri-theistic, even though it may be claimed that the godhood over against the created order is held to be the primary perspective. It has, however, as high a Christology as is possible with reference to God and has also a clearly unique doctrine of Jesus Christ as God

[4] Such a view would have been almost impossible to hold if either the definition of *persona* of Boethius or Aquinas, seven centuries later, had been kept in mind: *natura rationabilis individua substantia* or *persona individua est in se subsistens, ab aliquis separata.* Cf. also D. M. Baillie: "Thus in the sense in which we speak of ourselves as persons, it is truer to think of God as one Person, than as three" (*God Was in Christ,* p. 136).

[5] This view is, of course, unbiblical. Jesus spoke of the Father in him and of the Father doing his works!

[6] Cf. Gregory of Nyssa, *Why We Do Not Believe in Three Gods.*

and Savior. Its lack is with regard to the full humanity of
Jesus. Jesus, in this view, was no human personality. He had
no full, essential and permanent human nature.

The view that God became incarnate *in* Jesus, on the other
hand, starts with no view of God. Neither does it start with
any view of man. It starts with Jesus as the historic manifestation of Agape. He is a person in history among other
persons. But by seeing him we see through to God. We see
God through him because He was in him. The fundamental
fact is that God is of such a nature, and man is, too, that
they can co-exist without there being two egos. In one personality God and man are present together so as to form one
ego, all the more unified and real for being together. The
more fully and fulfillingly God and man co-exist in man
the more man is man. The one God is of such a nature as to
become incarnate. If He was truly present in Jesus while
still being Himself, God is both transcendent and becomes
immanent in man. Since personalities are unique and at
inmost are noncongruent, the one personal God remains
forever transcendent, uniquely Himself, even while becoming
incarnate by co-inherence, or interpenetration, as Spirit.[7] God
is transcendent, we say, as *personal* Spirit and incarnate as
personal *Spirit.* Such are the natures of both personality
and spirit.

The clue to the doctrine of the Trinity is, therefore, that
God is not a spiritual Personality but a personal Spirit. If
the word "Trinity" is to belong within the context of reality

[7] The fuller explanation of Spirit we saw, of course, in chap. 2.

as seen from the starting point of Jesus as Agape, it means that God Himself, the Father, as such never becomes incarnate. The eternal personal self-being of God remains forever transcendent over His every creation. God is Father. But God is also the outgoing Spirit who creates and redeems. Seen in the singularity of Son, conclusively self-revealed in the historic Jesus, the Godhead discloses His ultimate unity in oneness. Seen in the plurality of the Church, God expresses the ultimate creative diversity of the Godhead. God as personal Spirit has manifested Himself thus in love for the world.[8] Thus God is and loves. The Trinity, then, is the way we understand God as personal Spirit, by nature both transcendent and becoming incarnate, and in the broadest sense of the nature of Spirit, immanent.

Jesus is then related to the Trinity in terms of the pre-existent Son. The pre-existent Son is God Himself in His outgoing capacity as Spirit, operating in the singular.[9] This Son ever is with God and is God. The eternal Son it is who

---

[8] "But if he moves himself, and is not moved by need, what else can move him but love. For love finds its satisfactions within and not without" (Kierkegaard, *Philosophical Fragments,* p. 18). Need can be defined relationally and thus God has no need. He is the Fount of Reality. He is the full Source. He is the overflowing Origin. But need can also be defined within the context of God. In this case God needs to love because it is His self-sufficient nature to do so. Need to love is then an expression of the perfection of God. In such a case God finds satisfaction both within and without, but is never dependent upon satisfaction from without. Nevertheless, our response to God's love matters to God and gives Him satisfaction within His own self-sufficient Love.

[9] This definition is concretely ontological, stemming from God's actual revelation of Himself as the personal Spirit who is holy Love. It is not operational in the economic or modal sense.

is begotten, not made.[10] Von Speyer has rightly written that
"as the beginning, God declares *that* he is. As the word, he
declares *who he is*."[11] Before the Incarnation the relation
of the Trinity to Jesus was one of potentiality. Jesus as
Jesus did not exist; but He who was to form the regulative
reality of Jesus did. How, however, did this Son become
related to Jesus in the Incarnation?

In this relation is contained the mystery of God's relation
to man, of the Infinite to the finite, of the Sinless to the
sinful. In some sense the Eternal must remain in eternity, in
God's time, while still entering human time. In some sense
He must remain God, even while incarnate, retaining His
fullness. In another sense, He must accommodate Himself
to the mode of finite man. The very nature of God, we
repeat, is to be personal Spirit who as *personal* Spirit remains
invariably Himself while as personal *Spirit* He condescends
to the nature of the creature. Such condescension is the
mystery of *kenosis,* the divine self-emptying.

The Godward side of the incarnate Son participated in the
Trinity, in the full personal Spirit of Agape who God is; the
manward side of the incarnate Son became, however, passive
to the human personality. Activity from the Godward side of
the incarnate Son was offered to Jesus through the passive

---

[10] A fascinating discussion of the historical development of this problem
is found in Wolfson's *The Philosophy of the Church Fathers,* Pt. Two, "The
Trinity, The Logos, and the Platonic Ideas," especially in the following
chapters: VII, "Origin of the Trinitarian Formula"; VIII, "The Holy Spirit
as the Pre-existent Christ"; IX, "The Holy Spirit as Begotten of Jesus";
X, "Identification of the *Logos* and the Holy Spirit"; and XI, "Differentiation of *Logos* and Spirit."

[11] *Op. cit.,* p. 14.

nature of God in man. Thus God the infinite, wholly loving and perfectly holy, was decisively present in Jesus. It was God who came, became incarnate, became flesh, became enmanned. It was God who came as Son, performed history's conclusive and finally saving miracle, the Christ-deed. God had taken the initiative and had been accepted. The human nature, on the other hand, had become pliable to the divine for which it was made. The human personality of Jesus had experienced God's initiative in "sending" [12] His Son. This initiative was partly taken through human history, especially through "the Israel of God" and through the Holy Family. We cannot know, for instance, how decisive may have been the part taken by Mary herself. In a true sense, because of this transmissive initiative by which God enters man, Mary can rightly be called the Mother of God. *Theotokos* has an honored history and contains a holy truth. The initiative was supremely taken by the Holy Spirit. When the Son became incarnate, however, He became so primarily only by the direct initiative of God. God as the personal Holy Spirit alone can procreate the eternal Son in human history. In this sense Jesus was truly conceived of the Holy Spirit and in this sense the Virgin Birth expresses a definitive fact. God Himself, the Father, thrusts Himself as Son into a pliant human

[12] Obviously, in one sense, such language is symbolic. Roger Shinn feels that there is a subtle inconsistency between the ontological and the symbolic language. I dare not suggest a rupture in the ultimate unity of God, and yet basic to my understanding of God as Spirit is His capacity both to be Himself and also to become differentiated and identified with what is not Himself. This is the reason I feel justified in using language that may seem tri-theistic. I believe that the Bible basically is not tri-theistic even while using language of this kind.

being, whatever human struggles made active such passivity to God. But He did so also necessarily as the Source and Creator of Community, as the Holy Spirit.

The Godward side of the incarnate Son remained fully God, while acting, as Spirit does, on the manward side, on the passive side of God the incarnate Son. Divine perfection, power and sinlessness were thus present in Jesus or else he could not have incarnated the Son of God. The side of the incarnate Son that remained actively fully God offered itself continually through the passive side of the incarnate Son to the passive depth nature of the human personality of Jesus for his active response. God never forces Himself on man. Within his measure of freedom, man is inviolably free. Yet God is present as power for incentive and choice. The more man receives God in freedom the more powerful this presence of God in him becomes.[13] In Jesus the presence and power of God became the regulative reality, as in freedom his active humanity became fulfillingly pliant to the divine presence. In this way the passivity of God in Jesus became fulfillingly controlled by the active will of God. The presence of God became enmanned as the controlling reality through freedom, thus unifying *and making more real* the human personality of Jesus. Thus the personal Spirit, who God is, interpenetrated and fulfilled the human nature of Jesus. Jesus by being conclusively Son of God became decisively Son of Man in the fullness of human time as well

[13] Richard Baxter knew how much incentive sprang from the love that never violates man's freedom: "A man must heartily love God above all before he can heartily serve Him before all" (*The Reformed Pastor*, p. 73).

as in the fullness of divine time. God is the personal Spirit who is holy Love, and when He as personal Spirit became present fulfillingly in Jesus' personality, God as very God entered human nature and human history through the very way human nature and history are destined to be made. Therefore in Jesus Christ we meet very God and very man without separation and without confusion, in no "third Word," to cite Barth, or in no third Being as the Fathers put it, but in a real personality of human history, Jesus the Christ, the Son of God and the Son of Man.

This offering of the active will of God through the passive will of God happens below the level of conscious knowledge or choice. Thus God's presence can be indirectly rejected, ignored or accepted. Human freedom is preserved. Nothing of human nature is destroyed or truncated. In the depths is the creative nothingness of God. It is neutral territory, a no-man's-land for the exchange of ideas and suggestions. "In silence the soul becomes the womb for the Word." [14] In the depths there is indirection of communication. It is the divine light shining in the darkness and man seeing through the darkness mostly as he wills to see. God is present with man and for man, but not of man or integrally in man until man accepts and understands, and understands and accepts, the nature and way of God. Such is man's response in love to Love, for it is the very nature of love to transcend its own point of view, correctingly and fulfillingly.

[14] Von Speyer, *op. cit.*, p. 30. Or Rilke has put it that silence is the heart-soil for the seedbed of thought.

Therefore Jesus, being fully human, could be tempted even while the Holy Spirit was fully present.[15] God cannot be tempted. It is a deep wrong to make such a claim. Nor does God lead men into temptation directly. God as God is never the Tempted. But He can let even Jesus be tempted by his nature and by his environment; and yet sustain him in his temptation by the decisive offering of Himself. Such presence is no determining reality. Jesus was still free to sin. He overcame signally, rather, because his humanity was invitingly porous to God's empowering presence in him. Thus he was tempted as man, but overcame as both God and man, especially as the Godman. God, too, was present while Jesus was tempted, present with finitude and ignorance without thereby becoming limited Himself; and without thereby making the humanity of Jesus infinite and all knowing. Jesus could differentiate between his own knowledge and God's [16] without thereby denying that in his deepest spirit or in his fullest reality he and the Father were one.[17]

We can also begin to understand how the sinless Son of

[15] Luke 4:1.

[16] Notice that I say *"could"* differentiate, not *"did"* differentiate. There is doubt concerning the authenticity of the "I" passages in John. They do not sound like the voice of the Jesus of the Synoptic Gospels. On the other hand, I believe that Jesus felt, in his depth-self, his identity with God as Agape, particularly revealed, perhaps, by his humble, seeming denial of the fact, as in his retort "Why do you call me good? No one is good but God alone." Therefore I believe that at least such a statement could have been made of him, and that, for all we know, Jesus *was* humbly aware of God's very presence in him. Such a statement is thoroughly un-Jewish, but then the effect of Jesus' life caused a break with Judaism.

[17] Again cf.: "He is not only God's electing of man but man's choosing God. Jesus Christ is not only God's freedom for man but man's freedom

God could be truly present in Jesus without denying that God in Christ actually assumed and conquered our sins. Jesus was both the incarnation of Him who cannot sin and yet knew the inner reality of sin as the *acceptance* of anxiety. During his lifetime he knew both the fear that made him cry unto God day and night [18] and the perfect Love that throws out fear.[19] The ego of Jesus was not split nor were there two egos in him. The human drive of the ego was within the anxieties and conflicts of the world, knowing tensions to the point of groans and open conflict all the way to cold sweat that felt like blood, but the personality of Jesus was so integrally related to, and expressive of, God's own presence that the anxiety was dissolved and the temptations were signally conquered, so much so that Jesus experienced the ministration of angels. We need deny neither that God as Son assumed our sins in Jesus Christ nor that He effectively conquered them and made a living way for us to overcome sin and come before God's throne of grace with boldness.

The eternal Son of God in Jesus both assumed man's sin—

---

for God. The man who chooses, repents and trusts is Jesus" (Cochrane, *The Existentialists and God,* p. 45). Cf. also T. F. Torrance: "The Incarnation shows us that revelation is not only act of God in man and from the side of man, but real act of man achieved through human obedience to the Word of God. The Incarnation was wholly act of God but it was no less true human life truly lived in our actual humanity. Jesus Christ is not only Word of God to man, but Believer" (in T. H. L. Parker, *op. cit.,* p. 16).

[18] Heb. 5:7.

[19] I John 4:18. For an opposite interpretation of this subject, cf. Berkouwer, *The Person of Christ,* chap. X, "The Sinlessness of Christ."

that is Jesus accepted and knew anxiety—and also became conclusively regnant over sin in Jesus. How else could Agape become freely and arrestingly central in his life and through his life to history? If by sinlessness is meant such *conclusive* victory of Agape in Jesus' life, the concept is needed first because it is historical and secondly because it is redemptive. Such a view never obstructs the true interpretation of God's assumption of our sins, in Jesus and in us, and it never denies the full, ordinary humanity of Jesus. Much demand for Jesus' sinlessness springs out of our longing for a perfect man and for a false view that God cannot co-inhabit a sinful nature. The Christian faith, rather, glories precisely in God's actual assumption of our sins by His identification with the sinner against sin. In Jesus this identification was conclusive enough and freely enough received to let Agape become conclusive in his life. Thus God became fulfillingly central to human history, awaiting a similar consummation in succeeding history.

In Jesus, God assumed and knew our finitude, ignorance and sin essentially. The reasons that we hold this position, as we have seen, are biblical, historical and experiential. The union of God and man in Jesus Christ both expressed the purpose of God and fulfilled the nature of man. We have in Jesus, as Vincent Taylor holds, our true representative. His humanity makes God's presence real and relevant to us. He is the exceptional Event that transformingly fulfills, clarifies and transforms the past and, as history's center, offers a full Gospel for all mankind.[20] The exceptional Event exemplifies the potential nature of man and our eventual relation to God. God has Himself come in Jesus Christ that eternity might be born in the midst of time and perfect holiness might wipe away man's sinfulness.

Before the Incarnation the eternal Son of God had only a potential relation to Jesus.[21] Jesus as a human personality came into being within the span of human history, but he accepted the eternal Son as the constitutive reality of his personality. After Jesus died his humanity remained. Beyond death, Jesus is still the Godman. His humanity is affixed, to be sure, to the Trinity through the dominant, integral reality of the eternal Son. Jesus is, then, decisively more God than man, for God and man are incommensurable relations; but the humanity not only remains, but is subject to eternal growth in grace. The human can never catch up with, and exhaust, the divine. Man can never reach God. We never then use the word "Jesus" as though he ever was or ever became the *eternal* Son. We cannot pray to him as God. He is forever the Son of God in glory, with a create humanity dependent for its continued fulfillment on the uncreate God who as Son forms and fills full his humanity.

[20] Cf. a suggestive statement from Berdyaev: *"That higher creative, positive being, though unattainable at the time when redemption was begun, when God was still transcendent to man, is attainable in another period of religious life, after the redemption, when God in man is immanent"* (italics in the text). *The Meaning of the Creative Act*, p. 105.

[21] Cf. C. E. B. Cranfield's investigation of the Bible on the subject: "That it is the pre-existence of the Divine Subject of the Incarnation and not the pre-existence of Jesus Christ as man that is meant is fairly clear" (in Parker, *op. cit.*, p. 80).

The eternal purpose which God purposed before the creation of the world is thus fulfilled in Jesus as the Christ, the center of history, the usherer in of a new and final stage.

II. GOD AND HUMANITY

We now turn to the question of the relation between Jesus and us. Our chapter topic includes Jesus and the rest of humanity on the human level, and Christ and the Christian on the divine. We have discussed our first point: God and Jesus. The fact is that in Jesus Christ the eternal Son of God has come into human form and into human history. The eternal, ontological Son, the pre-existent personal Word, is Agape, the personal Spirit who is wholly Love and holy Love. The Son denotes particularly the eternal structural singularity of God. In the fullness of time in a human being, in Jesus of Nazareth, the Word became flesh, fulfilling His previous operational, subagapaic presence in human history, particularly in the Hebrew prophets and in the Israel of God.[22] In Jesus both incognito and clearly, the Word was and spoke. The human form delivered the divine Presence within the relativities and fallibilities of human existence; the deity of Agape presented the nature of God in the self-contained pattern of revelation for those who have eyes to see Him because they have hearts to accept Him. Henry Moore, the Cambridge Platonist, uttered a cardinal fact for

---

[22] God is never subagapaic in Himself, but He *operates* as such peda-gogically in preparatory human history and personality. Cf. my *Christianity and Society,* sec. II, "The Church and the World."

knowing when he asserted that only if thou beest it, thou seest it!

When the disciples came to understand and to accept who Jesus was, and when the community of the Christian people was born on Pentecost, the Holy Spirit became revealed to human history. He is the eternally plural in God. As Von Speyer has it: "The Holy Spirit is the eternal unity of those who meet eternally in love." [23] Augustine knew that the Holy Spirit relates the Father to the Son, the Self-existent One to the outgoing, creating, redeeming, relational One. The Holy Spirit also relates man to God through God Himself in the fullness of time. Such a relation was first consummated in the incarnate Son when the eternal Word fulfilled organically and made one personality of Jesus Christ, fully human and yet constitutively enmanning the very God of eternity. In both the instances of the singularity and the plurality of God come to earth, God was present so as to fulfill and not to destroy the humanity, whether singly or communally. The perfection was of God, truly and observably present, but not so as to destroy the ordinary humanity, singular or plural, or our sinful natures. In both instances, rather, the sinful nature was taken up into, transformed, redeemed and made victorious by the imperial presence of the ever-faithful God.[24]

[23] *Op. cit.*, p. 22.

[24] In this sense we understand Athanasius' statement: "He was made man that we might be made God" (Hardy, *op. cit.*, p. 107), or as the translator points out in the literal translation: "He was humanized that we might be deified."

The Son and the Holy Spirit are hereafter the standards and the motivational dynamic for true humanity, not as discarnate persons, individually or collectively, but as incarnate within our very real humanity. The light of the Incarnation is both clear and yet concealed. It comes to us truly judging and promising salvation, if we but will, and yet also hidden within our situation that the Word might be both real and relevant to us.[25] In Jesus Christ has come, in life, word, act and event, the fullness of God as Agape, offering a personal life that lives completely a universal, creative and saving Love; and in the Church has come the inclusive, unconditional Love, who God is, in the Holy Spirit, offering us fulfillment of community within our collective nature. Thus both the Son and the Holy Spirit, in incarnate form, are offered to us for our salvation, hitting our lives right where we are. We cannot have one without the other. No full surrender to God as Son will do, no personal acceptance of God without an unqualified receiving of the Holy Spirit, the surrender to the baptism of a new community, the Church. Nor can we receive the Holy Spirit from God and in relation to the Church without an unqualified surrender to, and acceptance of, the Son who speaks uniquely to our sinful state before God. No more personal or communitarian categories can be found than the Son of God and the Holy Spirit.

In the sense that Jesus Christ is the Incarnation of God

---

[25] For an excellent discussion of this topic, see Berkouwer, *op. cit.*, chap. 13, "Christ Incognito?"

as Son, and in the sense that the Holy Spirit is the Incarnation of God in His communitarian capacity, both Jesus Christ and the Church stand unbridgeably beyond us, judging us. Here has come the revelation that man can never understand nor receive in himself, for God can neither be known nor accepted except in terms of His own presence to communicate Himself and to save. In this all-important sense, both Jesus Christ as Son of God and the Holy Spirit in the Church are God's presence and power; and they are not at our natural disposal. Both, as such, are uncreate and forever beyond us as human beings; we can never become God individually or collectively.

While we remain sinners, then, or until we become new beings, we are qualitatively distinct from Jesus Christ as the victorious Godman. Sin stands between us and Jesus Christ negatively as does our lack of a positive relation of nature, our lack of the new Being. As human beings, furthermore, we are forever apart from both the eternal Son and the eternal Holy Spirit. We never can become God.[26] We shall always remain derived and dependent creatures, even though children of God. Or, to put it another way, the human personalities of our created spirits can never become part of the Trinity. The Trinity is God in His eternal self-being as Father; His eternal outgoing as creative and redemptive Love, the singular Son; and His eternal outgoing

[26] In this sense I cannot follow the statements of the Fathers as to man's being made God.

Community, the Ground of the Holy Spirit. Thus we know God. If it is now said that such an understanding of the Trinity presupposes understanding from within our relation to Him, we reply that only thus can we know God. The persons of the Trinity are operational capacities in God, as eternal as the God we know.[27]

We know no other God. We can never, should never, dare never think of God as self-sufficient *Being* apart from all creation after we know Him as Love in Jesus Christ. He is thereafter known as self-sufficient *Love* and only thus may we understand Him. Forever God is God, and never man. Berdyaev's theandric God or the Godmanhood means for us no more than that God is by nature creatively and redemptively outgoing toward man. God is with man and is man's true center. But God never becomes man in the sense that God stops being God. He only divests Himself of those actualities of presence that would destroy the manhood. He is Himself, rather, even in Incarnation with regard to and in relation to Himself, whether in the Son or in the Holy Spirit, even though He also accommodates Himself to

[27] Thomas Torrance has written that we cannot "get behind the back of Jesus to the eternal Son of God" (in T. H. L. Parker, *op. cit.,* pp. 15-16). If he means by this that we cannot go beyond the actual God as revealed, well and good. If He is ultimate to our understanding, how could we? If, however, he means that we cannot construct a creative understanding of God from God as revealed, we disagree categorically with him. It is the duty of Christian theology to understand all that we can concerning God, man and the world in the light of the revelation. It is only in such a way that the Church has come to any doctrine of the Holy Trinity. We need a doctrine of God that follows from the facts of the revelation in relation to all other facts, not doctrines that are *non sequitur.*

the conditions of humanity. Thus it is literally wrong to say with Irenaeus and Athanasius that God became human to make us divine. Our humanity never becomes divine; it remains eternally derived and dependent being.

III. Is Jesus Unique?

The basic question that is often asked is this: Is Jesus unique? This is our third topic. Many feel that unless he is, we have no ultimate revelation and no Savior. Over and over again it is said that the line must be drawn fundamentally between Christian heresy and orthodoxy, between those who hold Jesus to be basically one of us and those who hold him to be basically different from us. What have we to say on this crucial issue, clearly and directly?

Søren Kierkegaard puts the question succinctly. We have either a Socratic occasion or a Christian moment.[28] In the Socratic occasion the truth is general and detachable from the bearer of universal truth. Thus a teacher is the more able the more he himself falls into the background and allows the truth to speak for itself. The universal that he is

---

[28] "From the standpoint of the Socratic thought every point of departure in time is *eo ipso* accidental, an occasion, a vanishing moment. The teacher in himself is no more than this; and if he offers himself and his instruction on any other basis he does not give but takes away. . . ." (Kierkegaard, *op. cit.*, p. 6).

"The Moment makes its appearance when an eternal resolve comes into relation with an incommensurable occasion. Unless this is realized we shall be thrown back on Socrates, and shall then have neither God as Teacher, nor an eternal Purpose, nor the Moment" (*Ibid.*, p. 18). For a full discussion on this profound theme Kierkegaard himself must be studied.

advocating can be universally exemplified. Not so with the Christian moment where the Christ is indissolubly connected with the Christian message. The Christian Evangel is no universal truth concerning us, actually or potentially, but is, rather, the truth concerning Jesus as the Christ. There is only one Christ come to earth once for all, and therefore there can be no detaching of the Messenger from the message. He is universal in such a way that He remains the universal God precisely in such a manner that no one else can take His place. He has come once for all at a particular time in human history. He alone is God's redemptive truth for man, his way and his life. To reject Him is to remain in darkness and death; to accept and confess Him is to be delivered from darkness and death and to enter the realm of God's light and power. The Socratic occasion centers in a general truth; the Christian moment centers in a particular Person. Which of these two alternatives is true?

The answer is that neither is true. Both are false. Two dangers beset our dealing with Christ. The first is the reducing of Jesus to a human being in such a way that we have no final revelation of God. In that case Jesus is simply our best example in life; he is history's most high. This position is peculiarly pleasing to those who cannot abide the judgment of the Christ. If Jesus is simply one of us, we can admire him and we can follow him, but we cannot meet God in him and we cannot believe that God Himself has made a living way for us through Jesus to Himself. The other position is dealing with Jesus as God in a human body. Then, indeed, we have God present and we can believe in His mighty redemption. But, then, also we worship Jesus away from us.[29] If we cannot be as he was and walk even as he walked, then he is not fully real and relevant for us as human beings. Jesus himself knew that people always want to raise tombs for the prophets in order to hold them off in worship, even while killing the living prophets of God. We may either reduce Jesus into impotence or raise him into irrelevance.

True Christology, however, puts Jesus both at the edge and at the center of history. He is at the edge, for here history has been ended or, at least, fulfilled as *human* history. As God's presence on earth, Jesus stands ever in our van, beckoning us on, judging, changing and saving us. As God's presence in the midst of time, however, He also stands always at the center. In Him all things come together

[29] In order never to be guilty of such removal of Jesus Christ from humanity we never refer to him as God's only Son. Such a statement would cut Christology away from full relevance. God's only Son is the eternal pre-existent Word, who was in the beginning with God and was God. He is begotten before all ages. He is logically but not chronologically subsequent to the Father. There was no time when the Son was not. We repeat John of Damascus' affirmation that God was never wordless. This God as outgoing, creative and redemptive Love, or God structured and operating as Son, is the only begotten Son whom God sent, or the only-begotten *God*, as John 1:18 can be rendered with some manuscript support. Hardy points out how the simpler formula, "Christ Jesus, Son of God," was changed probably already by the end of the third century to read, "his only Son our Lord" (*op. cit.*, p. 16). The "only" causes no mischief if directed to God as Son. He and He alone is God's presence ontologically or historically as revealing and saving Son. The harm is done when "only" is applied to the humanity of Jesus in such a way that there must be a denial that the eternal Son is in all who are rightly related to God, that He and the Holy Spirit alone can fulfill and constitute man as true man and true community.

or hold together and are seen for what they are. He is both at the end of time, in our sense of it, awaiting our arrival to be with Him; and also at the center of time, enabling us to find who we are and what human existence means. He shows us, furthermore, how to repent of our sins and mistakes and how to find the power to become sons of God. Insofar as God as Agape in Jesus became conclusively expressed and active, we have here both history's goal for us and the meaning of history as seen from its own mid-point.

First, therefore, Jesus cannot be a Socratic occasion, for he is not merely a general truth. He is a personal Event. Athenagoras with insight called him Son of God in "his Word in idea and in actuality." [30] The Word as idea is generally meaningful to us, but as actuality that Word is concretely living, a personal Event. When time became full and finished as human time with his death and resurrection,[31] the once-for-all revelation of God had been made. Jesus is forever connected with this revelation. Here the miracle of time took place. The proclamation of the Gospel must forever be beyond all general truths and must be in terms of God's personal Christ-deed. In Jesus Christ we have the summit and the summary of human history. No other Absolute can come, for there is only one God, the uncreate,

---

[30] Richardson, ed., *Christian Fathers,* p. 309.

[31] "The Resurrection shows *par excellence* how Godhead and manhood have personally met together. This happens in the concrete and historical life of Jesus the Christ. But what happens is not limited by time and space. It changes time and space and has eternal consequences. History has a different direction and the destiny of man is changed" (Singh, *op. cit.,* p. 76).

eternal Lord.[32] Thus we speak in faith, not as those who can
know beyond what has been given to us. Those who have
seen the vision of all things coming together in Christ,
however, can make no less a statement. Whenever God
comes in fullness of time it is the time of Jesus Christ. It is
the same eternal Son and He comes to the same humanity.
Therefore Jesus is indissolubly connected with God as
Trinity, the singular Love expressed in Him and the communitarian Love expressed concerning Him in the Church.
Whenever God comes to us, it is as the Godhood of Jesus
Christ, the Agape Himself; wherever the true humanity is
effected, it is as the manhood of Jesus Christ, the human
nature within the organic power and fulfillment of the Word.

[32] In this sense we accept Emil Brunner's affirmation of the *Einmaligkeit*
of Jesus Christ in the first chapter of *The Mediator,* but never in the sense
that the absolute cannot come again into human history. It is not the once-
for-allness that counts in terms of time but the once-for-allness in terms
of eternal Being—God as Agape. In *Eternal Hope* Brunner complains that
I have misunderstood him at this point. This book might clear the issue
between us. We reject consequently outright Mascall's argument in *Christian
Theology and Natural Science* that the eternal can take on human form only
once because such a union becomes unique and unrepeatable. In such a
case He who came in Jesus had thereby exhausted His possibilities for
coming by committing Himself concretely to man once for all. Thus to
teach is to deny that Christ and the Holy Spirit are both to dwell in us
and make us full as new creatures "with all the fulness of God." In
Mascall's previous terms, the divine "Who," I believe, is not limited to any
human "what." As a matter of fact, such language denies the Incarnation
where the "Who" is both divine and human within historic existence.
Mascall's putting of the case: "The Word became man by assuming a human
nature which had no personal individuality of its own and, in assuming
it, he conferred his personal individuality upon it; if *per* [*par*] *impossible*
he assumed, and conferred his personal individuality upon human nature
twice over, there would not after all be two individuals but only one; which
is simply a paradoxical way of saying that in fact human nature could not
be assumed by the divine Word more than once, since it is individualised
in his Person and that Person is numerically one" (*ibid.,* p. 41).

But neither can Jesus Christ, on the other hand, be a Christian moment in the sense that he is "wholly other" and utterly different from us. Such a statement denies the Incarnation at its heart and, indeed, the whole purpose of the Incarnation, namely, to have God enter into our full human situation and actually become flesh in order that His experience might become part of our own experience, and to work our redemption from within in order to safeguard and to fill full our human freedom and reality. After all, Jesus Christ was *of* God and not *like* God; and he was *of* man and not *like* man. The Incarnation means that Jesus Christ was very God and very man—in no "third Word," as Karl Barth affirms, but as a true personality, of both God and man. There is a dynamic coming together of God in man, in a true relation, in Jesus Christ, in a *real personality,* not a substantive division or fusion of natures. After all, there is only one God as Son, one second Person in the Trinity; and there is only one kind of human nature, whether fallen or perfected. Christology is true relation, not an addition that makes Jesus different from us nor a subtraction from either true Godhood or true manhood. On this point the Church, in its main decisions, has been eloquently consistent.

We cannot separate Jesus from ourselves, then, either by addition or subtraction. We cannot deny that he was truly and fully human. Nor can we deny that God as Son, Christ Himself, must fulfill our human natures if we are to be

saved. Christ is in all saints "the hope of glory." If we have
not the Spirit of Christ, biblically, we are none of His. We
no longer live but Christ lives in us, and the life we live,
we live by faith in the Son of God. The New Testament
fairly shouts at us the fact that Christ is our new life, that
we are new creatures in Christ. He was full of grace and
truth, and of His fullness *we all received,* grace for grace.
In Him dwells all the fullness of God bodily and *in Him
we are made full.* When we are rooted and grounded in
love and Christ dwells in our heart by faith, then we, too,
can expect to become filled with all the fullness of God.
Each man is to be presented perfect in Christ; and we all
are to come to the measure of the stature of the fullness
of Christ. The Early Church Fathers also rang all the changes
on this theme and Luther, Calvin and Butzer agreed on the
actual presence of Christ in his Church whether, as in
Luther's interpretation, hidden behind the masks of God
(*larva dei*) or, as in Calvin's, seen with a clear countenance
(*vera facies*). If there is only one eternal Son, and if He
is in both Jesus and us, we cannot, in any case, make Jesus
unique by his having God in him as his very being. For
us to live as the new Being must mean that we also have the
same Son to fill the empty place at the middle of our lives.
If there is only one human nature, we cannot remove Jesus
from the saints either by his not having a human nature or
by our nature not being truly human. We must, rather, say
that he was the first fully human being, in that he was first
fully related in a conclusive sense to God as Son. Love once

broke into human history to fulfill man in Christ Jesus, and through him to fulfill all men. Such a statement is historic fact, with no minimizing of human fallibility and with no attempt to deny God's previous mighty presence and acts in history. In Jesus Christ, Agape became the distinctive and dominant fact of history, whatever be the relation to the fulfillment, clarification, transformation or revolution of all else in human history, and whatever be the need for fulfillment in future human history.

Is Jesus, then, in no sense unique? He is. Here heaven entered history; here eternity fulfilled time; here God became man; here the Word became flesh. These are actual affirmations of historic fact. The uniqueness of Jesus is the uniqueness of a historic fact, not of a relation to God inaccessible to anyone else. Agape became sufficiently regnant in his life, not only to clarify for us the meaning of God, not only to work a radical change in human history, but also to conquer death through resurrection.

We cannot say that Agape became victorious at once or to the point where there was no human struggle or failure. We may believe so, but neither the record nor the status of historic documents attest this to be the case. We cannot therefore appeal to the sinlessness of Jesus as a decisive differentiation between him and us.[33] If we could do so, then God never assumed our main plight from within and never

---

[33] We cannot accept especially Berkouwer's distinction between Jesus and us: that he alone had the inability to sin. No statement more directly denies the humanity of Jesus. *Op. cit.,* chap. 10.

won the victory through Incarnation.[34] At least in such a case He never won it from within our actual nature and situation. We believe, rather, that Jesus is the full assumption by God of our human predicament and His victory through him over it. The Bible is a far better guidebook than is any pseudo-orthodox theology that dares not really have Jesus growing in grace in the sight of God and men, that cannot accept at face value his own obviously original utterance (if we know any) that God alone is good and that therefore perfect goodness must not be ascribed to him, that must avoid the implications of his own prayer that included a petition for forgiveness, of his baptism unto the remission of sin, of his refusal as the sinless one who had to uphold the law to cast a stone on the woman taken in adultery, of his learning obedience through what he suffered and of his being made perfect, of the Sinless being made sin for us that we might be made the righteousness of God through him, of his acceptance of anxiety whereby instead of having the perfect love that casts out fear he sometimes demonstrated the fear that cried day and night unto him who was able to save him from death, and of his own crying out and moaning for tensions, as at the grave of Lazarus, indicating the acceptance of anxiety rather than the perfect poise of discarnate deity.

[34] Cf. Luther's statement: "Thus making a happy exchange with us, He took upon Him our sinful *person,* and gave unto us His innocent and victorious *person,* with which we are now clothed and are freed from the curse of the law" (W. A. 40/1, p. 443, in Torrance, *Kingdom and Church,* p. 38).

Some of these passages may be doubted on scholarly grounds, such as the woman taken in adultery, but they are far more reliable than isolated claims of sinlessness that may have sprung out of a theologizing about Jesus that already feared the full relevance of the Incarnation. Historically we start with a strong figure through whom history was changed by the volcanic eruption into the historic consciousness of the Agape of God. In all decisive instances of struggle, Jesus emerged the triumphant conqueror of anxiety, and angels ministered to him, whether after the temptations in the wilderness or in Gethsemane. Instead of an external, irrelevant theophany, we have the wondrous Incarnation of God Himself, assuming our whole burden of guilt in one for whom long and careful preparation had been made by God and who did not fail his task.

Some insist, moreover, on the biological Virgin Birth as the real sign of the supernatural Incarnation and as the point of permanent demarcation between Jesus and all others. We have already said that historically the case of critical scholarship stands generally against, rather than for, the Virgin Birth. There are nonetheless, on the other hand, no *a priori* reasons why God could not have come in such a way, and there certainly is also a historic strand on the positive side. The Virgin Birth, in any case, stands for the miraculous birth of the Son of God; it is pious adulation and should be honestly accepted as creative myth to adorn history's most significant Event. God comes only from God; He cannot be accounted for in terms of evolutionary development or of human continuity. To use the Virgin Birth, however, to separate Jesus by his very nature from the rest of humanity, is to destroy the central affirmation of the Incarnation. In such a case the Virgin Birth has already debased the full reality and relevance of Jesus' having a nature just like ours. It is hard, of course, for mankind to accept God's coming into human history inconspicuously and ordinarily. In our desire to honor Him we must create the stage of the coming of a king. God chose otherwise. His Son was of humble birth and became known by what He was, did and said. The uniqueness of Jesus, therefore, should not be laid at the door either of sinlessness or of the Virgin Birth. In this case the careful head sees more deeply into God's way of working than does the adoring heart that embroiders history to keep it from being understood within the planned plainness of God's way of coming.

In the case of the Resurrection, however, we have strong historic ground for believing it; and the Resurrection is also the result of the true hypostatic union. It consummated demonstrably history's unique union of God and man, for here history became fullness of time. God let Jesus return from the grave, however it happened, to encourage his disciples and to make firm in history the founding of the community of Agape. Whatever tales are told of other resurrections, they have never been confirmed like his, nor are they in accord with the best we know of God's way of working. The fullness of time became evidenced by Jesus' resurrection from the dead. Paul could write that Jesus was designated Son of God by the Resurrection. Here is the fitting and proper climax of earthly Incarnation. Here heaven stooped into history and God signaled His supernatural presence. Here God turned the stream of history from near defeat to nascent victory. The fact that we now can know Resurrection reality and power in this life is due to the fact that God did not fail in His Christ-deed. We shall not know this reality and power in any great measure in this life, however, for full resurrection is a matter of the total man living beyond this body of death, both the death of sin and the death of nature.

If, however, we too are in the end to be resurrected beyond actual physical death, then Jesus' return is not *in essence* different from our future. He came back to his disciples for a special purpose, and that privilege perhaps will never be granted in such a fashion to anyone else. But the most important fact is not his earthly appearance, but the new kind of existence at the call of God wherein the power of death is vanquished. If we are to participate in the community of the Resurrected and be sons of the Resurrection, we find no uniqueness in principle in the resurrection. We see once more that the uniqueness is not a relation to God whereby Jesus differs from us, but a historic concrete Event into which we are invited to enter.

In what sense, then, is Jesus unique? We have Jesus as the first-born among many brethren; he is the first-born from the dead and the first-fruit among them that slept. In him came a new age; in him came a new way of being right with

God, the only way to be fully right. Therefore Jesus became the mediator of a new covenant within which we draw near to God. Jesus is to be understood in terms of God's own coming into human nature and into human history. Never before was God as Agape, the personal Spirit who is holy Love, fully understood and accepted within human nature and history. The fullness of God as Love became truly present in Jesus within the conditions of actual human nature and without violating human freedom. God identified Himself with man because He loved him; He prepared patiently for one who would identify himself with God as He is; the fullness of time came when God could thus become conclusively identified with man by means of man's identification with God. We repeat, almost as a formula of incarnation: God came to man because He loved him; He came in man, waiting for his free response, because He respected man.

Jesus, therefore, became the actual Mediator of the knowledge, the presence and the power of God to forgive and to change human nature and human history.[35] Whoever comes after him most likely comes through him. At least, if he should not come by means of the knowledge and power of Jesus Christ directly, as a new manifestation of the eternal Son, he would have to come to Jesus Christ as the full nature of God and man. Whether he knows of Jesus or not, who-

---

[35] In this sense we can accept Schleiermacher's claim that "it is indisputable that all Christians trace back to Christ the communion to which they belong" (*The Christian Faith,* English Translation of the Second German Edition, edited by H. R. Mackintosh and J. S. Stewart, p. 54).

ever comes into the right relationship to God, comes in fact
to Jesus Christ, to God as Agape. For this reason there is no
other name by which we must be saved, for there is only
one eternal Son and only one right relation of man to Him.
No other foundation can man lay, for the true foundation
was laid once for all in the fullness of time. Any building
correctly from then on can only be a building on, and adding
to, the true temple of God. There is for us no Virgin Birth
whereby we are born not of blood nor of the will of the
flesh nor of the will of man, but of God, that is not also
the same Virgin Birth as that of Jesus Christ. There is no
victory over sin into the full relation of God and man that
is not the same as the positive victory over sin of Jesus
Christ. In him, in the Godman, we believe, sin has been
conquered and defeated in principle and power once for all.
There is no resurrection from the dead that is not part of
the power of his resurrection and the outcome of the fellowship of his sufferings. In this case we are dealing not
with theory or myth but with the historic fact of the victorious life of Jesus Christ as the Son of God, attested to
by the crucifixion and the resurrection from the dead. What
happened in Jesus, as Bultmann stipulates, should be re-
peatable in us; the Incarnation becomes not historical but
historic, not *historisch,* but *geschichtlich.* Yet historic categories cannot contain the fullness of time, God's own
fulfilling presence and the world's only Savior. Eternity
fulfills history; God, man.

In the same way Jesus Christ becomes the standard for

all who have died before him—or later, for that matter, without knowing of him. They can never come into right relation with God without being rightly related to the Son and to the Holy Spirit as the singular and plural Love of God. Both individually and collectively all must be fulfilled through the reality of God that came with Jesus Christ. To be sure, they need never know the historic details of his earthly life. We do not know what part that will play in the heavenly places, or, for that matter, in the preparatory places beyond death. But we do know that God has come; and to be right with God and with man, all must become rightly related to Him through the reality of the Incarnation, that is, through God as outgoing love, in order that we might be "partakers of the divine nature" (II Pet. 1:4). There is no other way. When anyone becomes thus related, he becomes related to Jesus Christ *in re*. If God is really Agape, such is the case even in all possible existences on other planets or in universes existing unthinkable ages before the creation of ours or unimaginably beyond ours. Currently there is a good deal of discussion as to the relation of Jesus to life on other planets among Greek Orthodox as well as Roman Catholics and Protestants. We cannot, of course, tell about these existences from within our span of time and space. We can tell, however, that whatever salvation *ever* exists, it must be a matter of being right with God who is faithful Love. All existences, however unimaginably different from ours, are judged and fulfilled by the reality of God who is Agape. What that actually means our eyes have not seen nor our ears heard, even in Jesus Christ, in any comparison to the possible riches of God in previous creations. We may be less than grasshoppers to Einstein in our understanding of God's inexhaustible love in comparison to other possible existences. We believe, however, that in Jesus Christ God has disclosed His heart, even if only the smallest bit of His mind. The eternal Son whom we met in Christ and now meet in our experience is God Himself; and therefore we believe that in this criteriological sense Jesus Christ is the true arrow to the nature and will of God for all times and existences. Such is our grasp of the finality of God's revelation in Jesus as Agape.

Jesus is now rightly related to God, in one sense within the Trinity, in that God constitutes regulatively his nature as a human being "of the right hand of God." For this reason we no longer know Jesus "according to the flesh" but as the Spirit. In Jesus Christ God acted climactically to save the world. The same Lord as Spirit acts now both in heaven and on earth. We must therefore not worship Jesus as a human being who as to his humanity forever remains like us. Yet we worship through the human being the Incarnate Lord who is saving Love. The constitutive reality of the Christ-deed was and is Agape. Those who have made an idol of the human Jesus and believe in him simply as God walking on earth may feel in this analysis that they have lost the Savior. But if they are hurt they need to be hurt, for only thus can they be helped to understand and to accept the true Savior who was fully God and man. Not a human being, but only God by His organic presence in a human being can save.

Those, however, who will meet God the Son in Jesus Christ—the God who is ever inclusive and holy Love, the personal Spirit of eternity—may even now live in the presence of the God who became incarnate for our sake, bore sin for our sake, and raised Jesus for our sake. Accepting the Son as well as the Holy Spirit, they will be made whole within their own selves, and, being joined to the community of God's redemption, will go forth with "joy and peace in believing," increasingly to find their faith true and their salvation real. From them must come the quiet, irrepressible witness to the eternal Son of God, become incarnate, by whom, and by whom alone, we can be saved.

V

CHRIST AS CREATOR AND CONSUMMATOR

———

THE final chapter will be devoted to the cosmic Christ. The eternal Son we know only through the cosmic Christ. In the end, of course, as the Bible holds, even the Son will be subjected to the Father in order that God be all in all. Eternally God is who He is. His creative Love, however, becomes manifest against the light of an epoch. That light will at last be blended within the eternal glory that exceeds any human thought. The eternal creations of God's endless Love, however, are not for us to fathom, except as the transcendent reality that forever debars us from knowing as God knows. Even when we shall know as we are known, we shall know as creatures and children, not as the Uncreate Father.

The cosmic Christ is God's outgoing Love in the creation, supervision, redemption and consummation of our age.[1] The cosmic Christ is the true representative of the eternal Son. They are the same, of course, yet the *eternal* Christ is the

[1] Col.: 1.15-20 clearly presents Christ as the principle and power of cosmic coherence.

eternally begotten or the eternally "anointed." He alone is the only Son of the Father, while the *cosmic* Christ is the Son understood and accepted against the background of our cosmic age. The *historic* Christ, again, is the eternal Son revealed through the life and teachings, suffering and resurrection of Jesus Christ. God is ever all in all as Agape, but Agape becomes manifest as Son in the cosmic creation through the historic Incarnation.

Many will hesitate to make the cosmic Christ available for the interpretation as well as for the judgment and salvation of our age. They prefer to believe in him simply as Savior. They want him efficacious only with regard to the forgiveness of sin. At least they want to view Him in no other perspective. They feel that to explain our total creation and experience by Him is to reduce Him to a cosmic principle and to make of Him a "vain philosophy." They believe that the Gospel is more potent against the background of man's darkness than in the foreground of his understanding. They feel that faith must trust as much for light as for forgiveness and that it is not given to man to understand the unsearchable ways of God. The Agape of God, they rightly reason, is no "mere intellectual principle"; but from this fact they go on to dismiss the need for any seeing of the total ways of God with our world. They often go on even to the point of pronouncing such an attempt to be a presumptive covering up of man's deepest need for total redemption through faith. Kantonen, in a meeting of a Faith and Order commission preceding the international World Council of Churches gathering at Evanston, charged that the modern Christian world has seen two basic heresies: Hegelian rationalism and the turning of Agape into a cosmic principle.

The truth is, however, that Christ is the answer even to our seeing. We do not see the whole of reality, of course, but we see truly into its meaning, for Christ is the light of life. Christianity is not a mystery religion, however deep its final mysteries and however unattainable from God's full perspective. The Christian faith is the religion of *revelation,* a revelation through both creation and redemption, both of which presuppose for their full meaning incarnation, while, in turn, all three require the reality of the Resurrection, the final and total victory of God over all enemies of man. Even though the Christian faith can never become a philosophy, inasmuch as it is a living relation of God to man, nevertheless, the only true philosophy stems from its center. Agape is the truth as well as the way and the life. Therefore He alone affords the full perspective and power of a philosophy of life and a philosophy of the world. Christ, being the true light, alone illumines for the eyes of faith creation, history and their consummation.

I. CHRIST THE CREATOR

Christ as Agape, then, to begin with, throws light on the meaning of creation. Yngve Bohlin has written a book *Den korsfäste skaparen* (*The Crucified Creator*). Creation receives its meaning through the crucifixion. The whole meaning of creation hangs on why the Creator Himself had to be crucified. Christ, the self-giving of God Himself in and with man alone explains why there should be any creation at all. No other explanation can begin even to touch the full Christian reason for creation. Beyond Anselm's *Cur deus homo* (Why God man?) lies the question of why God as man had to be crucified. Crucifixion explains creation.

Our cosmic process is too bold and too fast not to need explaining. If things, to our best knowledge, had always been much as they are, we should have no need, nor right, to try to explain them. Then we should only have to accept our order as fact and try to adjust ourselves to its nature. Instead, our cosmic process is only a few billion years old. The mere time span, however, is unimportant, except for the fact that things as we know them have not always been as they are, but have come to be. What matters far more is the fact that this cosmic process exhibits an incredible and unexplainable change of pace. Natural evolution was comparatively slow. Even the beginnings of life and of human life have been comparatively slow. But like a rocket in the middle of a pitchblack night has zoomed into being our history of humanity.

On the scale of three billion years' being thirty days, one thousand years is but a cosmic second. Human history, in any developed sense, is on such a scale but the ticking away of less than a handful of cosmic seconds. Two cosmic seconds ago Jesus came. The last tenth of a second has seen a revolutionized world, and the last hundredth of a second has ushered in a qualitatively new era. Whence this cosmic spurt? Whence this cosmic "blitz emergence"?

From the point of view of everything that is of basic importance and of communicable meaning history exhibits a leap, a chasm, a discontinuity of pace that defies all reason from within the process itself. The swift, accumulative series of novelties organically fulfilling one another in terms of life and meaning bespeak a Reality from *beyond our process* that controls creation and continues it. Christ as the most important and most meaningful event, the all-inclusive Love of God that needs a pedagogical process by its very nature and for purposes intrinsic to it, is the fullest answer to the reason for creation and to the nature of creation.[2]

The same answer holds good for those who point to a finite God as explanation for the cosmic process and for human history. The God who is seen as finite in terms of the results of the process cannot explain the process. If present results are the standard of truth, if a systematic analysis of the good and the bad in the world now—in other words, if a comprehensive coherence based on the world we actually know now—be the approach to the reality and nature of God, the God we find as a result is the God of the process and not the God who makes, supervises and completes the process. The cosmic surge is inexplicable in

---

[2] See my *Faith and Reason*, chap. 4, and *Christian Faith and Higher Education*, chap. 4. If it were not for such unexplainable cosmic change of pace, I should follow Whitehead in much more of my philosophy. Daniel Day Williams is one of our ablest interpreters of the theological adequacy of Alfred North Whitehead at this point, but as far as I can see, the classical Christian assumptions are even more adequate in this bewildering region of eternity and cosmic process.

terms of such a God. Who made Him leap into such sudden growth? The lightning-quick appearance of human history defies interpretation in terms of a God who is measured by the process as a whole as it now stands. No such measurement validly or adequately indicates the reason for the process and for the flash emergence of human history. When man freezes history he cannot find God!

The evidence is, rather, of a flaming arrow against the black sky, lighting up for our brief inspection, if we have eyes to see, a cosmic process being pulled by that arrow, against strong eddies of resistance. Evil, ignorance, sin, finitude and incompleteness combine to work as contrary forces to obscure or dim the main direction of the process. Thus only for those who hold the arrow in firm and fervent sight is there discernible a total movement, an over-all pattern of process distinct enough to convince them that the meaning and end of the arrow's flight are beyond our best hoping and beyond our most imaginative seeing.

For those who both will to see and study to see, there can emerge a pattern of process that is seen to be pedagogical in nature. Although we are baffled by slow beginnings and with slow starts, and although our faith has to be content with the heavy burden of contrary evidence even in the midst of human history, there *is* real unity to the universe, there *is* human history, and there *is* the truth of the Gospel. If the house of history were more bad than good it would collapse entirely. As men willingly, understandingly and lovingly come to grasp the meaning of life and of history, namely, that each person for himself and all together might come to find God real and humanity perfected only in Him, they see that history exhibits more than an "irony" whereby events conspire to an end. They see that, in fact, it gives evidence of being the appropriate setting, at its lowliest beginnings, of the eternal purpose God Himself has purposed in Jesus Christ.

All of life, then, becomes God's school, for decision and for information; and earthly life itself becomes but the one room in God's spacious school, where death is promotion or demotion to an unknown schoolroom and to a different kind of teaching. Only when life is seen from the focus of the furthest future, can it be viewed aright. What eventually is to be, as indicated by the flaming arrow, alone tells us, however dimly, what now is. The mystery of the Gospel is the only key to the mystery of life. Christ as the Omega alone reveals Christ the Alpha. Christ as the End is the only clue to Christ the Beginning. Christ the final Savior is the truest decipherer of Christ the Creator. And both Christ the Beginning and Christ the End are known to us in Jesus Christ as Christ the Center.

No understanding of why there should be any nature and any history at all can be accepted unless it dare to meet head on the problem of evil.[3] Why, after all, should there be this

---

[3] This is the reason that impelled me to write *Evil and the Christian Faith* even before a Christology. For a first-rate criticism of the Christian theologians' traditional treatment of evil, see J. L. Mackie, "Evil and Omnipotence," *Mind,* LXIV (1955).

kind of world, if the meaning of existence is God's sharing His perfect love? The answer of the Christian faith is simple and forthright. Evil can be understood and done away with only by the Cross of Christ. In order to have us free, God put us in an environment where we must learn indirectly. He measured the depth of our freedom by the abyss of His own suffering. God values man's freedom more than we can comprehend; He never violates it. Otherwise He would not have paid so much for it! The slow pace with which He starts and the thoroughness of the process by which He trains us terrifies us and often makes us lose both heart and faith. Only in the light of a time span, therefore, where our suffering is "but for a moment," biblically speaking, can we understand the ultimate value of freedom beyond its heavy cost.

Love's way is to bestow freedom and to redeem freedom by suffering. Such suffering is in human time. Yet as perfect compensation Love has eternity to offer those who have suffered and won. Love's suffering, too, has within its own heart the joy of identification with the beloved. Such joy is in the suffering of self-giving love, in being with the sufferer as a companion, and in the final victory over the suffering itself. The Cross answers the problem of moral evil partly in terms of the stubbornness of sin that shows the depth of man's freedom. For those who live and look in the light of the Cross—even while, to be sure, many problems of creation are dark with shadows—the central area is bright with meaning and shining with challenge. When creation is approached in the light of the Cross, the crucified Creator, there is at least no need to evade the problem of moral evil.

Natural evil also finds its meaning in the light of the Cross. God's means of teaching consist mostly in the indirect ways by which He proposes His answers to us in terms of the consequences we experience from various kinds of actions. The steadfastness of nature, for instance, can teach us initiative and responsibility. The fickleness of nature, on the other hand, can teach us to find our satisfactions beyond nature even more than in nature. The stern side of nature tempers us; its mild side makes us at home in it. Beyond both its sternness and its mildness, however, lie the severity and goodness of its Maker. Nature is neither a bed of roses nor a nest of rattlesnakes. It is neither populated entirely with lions nor entirely with lambs. Nature is both kind to life and blind to death. Within such mixtures one can certainly see no clear pattern for life and hope. Yet, even so, when the Cross, with its fuller meaning, and the Resurrection, with its endless span, light up the double-sidedness of nature, there emerges, for those who are willing and able to see, a secondary pattern of conditions for creative life that clarifies the main pattern of the Christ. Both moral and natural evil find an authentic approach to their solution in Christ the crucified Creator.

Christ as Creator becomes understood only in terms of Christ the Consummator. He who himself became cursed for our sake lets nature be similarly cursed. The "curse" of nature is put on it purposefully by its faithful Creator who will at the end remove its curse and reveal its hidden splendor. Nature is a faithful servant performing for a large part, as Luther put it, "the alien works of God." There is no evil in nature as such. The mosquito and the serpent, the goldenrod and the briar bush, the earthquake and the killing frost are not evil in themselves. They hurt us who cannot be helped apart from our being hurt. In God's way and day, however, the veil of God's "dark purpose" will be lifted and those who now hurt us for our help will join the morning stars and the sons of God in singing glory to the Creator. Nature's groans will turn to shouts of joy in the day of its full redemption. Then Christ the Creator whose face we now see in such deep shadows will appear as Christ the glorious Consummator of all things. Nature cursed will become nature glorified because Christ the Creator is none other than Christ the Consummator. The crucified Creator will at last consummate all nature.

II. Christ, the Lord of History

Christ, the Creator, is also Lord of history. Christ, as we have kept emphasizing for our purpose of interpretation, is the manward side of God. He is the Word made flesh, the eternal Son of the Father, God as Son, going out to create, to bring order and to save. The Christian faith is characterized by the fact that the cosmic Christ is revealed in the historic Christ, Christ the Creator in the Christ of history.

History is, of course, not to be understood as separated from nature. History belongs in part to the order of creation and in part to the order of redemption. As general providence, history is on the level of creation; as special providence, history is on the level of redemption; as sanctification, moreover, history is even on the level of resurrection. Redemption and resurrection, however, remain enmanned and therefore organically connected with the order of creation. History is, so to speak, cradled in the order of creation.

Christ works through the order of nature in history mostly through man's needs, or, rather, through his ability to satisfy those needs and through the means invented to satisfy those needs. Man has needs. He tries to answer those needs by means of nature, whether through *finding* in it food and shelter, or whether by *producing* the answers to his needs in terms of the development of his instruments to use nature. With such development the range of his community also grows. He thus learns gradually a complicated form of co-operation called the division of labor. As man's needs keep growing, physically, socially and mentally, man must keep growing with them in order to meet them and in order to find the fuller answer to their meaning.

Religion is man's answer to his deepest and longest needs. Man's religious answers are as complicated as his history of development; and they are as twisted in and around this history as his thinking is practical and flexible in relation to concrete situations. Christ the Creator has made a nature

233

that can be thus employed for man's good and for his increasing use. Christ the Creator has also made man able to exploit the natural resources, to invent better ways of using them and grow in understanding and range of vision with such mastery.

The Christ of history is thus working from underneath man to shove him along into new ways of living and into larger areas of activity. The Christ of history is on the side of nature as Christ the Creator. There he moves man along by means of his needs, by means of his capacity to meet those needs and by means of his growing problems connected with the enlarging process of meeting those needs. Man meets in this way an ever-expanding community. As his social horizons push out, he dwells also under a higher sky. Christ the Creator is thus a mainspring of history from below in terms of man's relation to nature and his material needs.

The Christ of history, however, operates also from above and before the historic process. He is Christ the Redeemer, who walks ahead of His people as they cross the wilderness of history on their way to the Promised Land. Christ comes through the pillar of fire to those who have been set on fire by His Love. He comes as the cloud of mercy in those who have found the divine power to be merciful. Through prophets and saints He comes, moving ahead of His people, luring them toward their goal. In spite of complaint, in spite of idolatry, in spite of defection and rebellion, on move the Pillar of Fire and the Cloud of Mercy. They move on until the Son who is the Sun rise on the horizon of human history. Then the Christ of history rises to the zenith of history. The summit of history is its potential center. All movement forward, from then on, can only be movement inward. All movement ahead thereafter can only be movement toward the center.

After Christ the Center of history has come, there can be only one way for history to go—His! All other paths mislead and carry to destruction. Christ the Center of history gives to history the context of God. He flings out against the darkness of human misery and ignorance the pattern of Calvary. History becomes forever marked by a Cross. The Cross breaks the circles of civilizations as they move on in endless variations of repetition from birth to death. The Cross gives a definite and fixed direction to history. Yet history does not run on, without running in toward the center. It does not run ahead except as all points of the circle named "ahead" mean in fact "toward the center." The coming of Christ the Center nevertheless does not mean that history is done because the fullness has come. The coming of the Center entails rather the absolute command to proceed at the fastest possible rate toward that center. History does not become still, but only more mobile, when the fixed point of God's final purpose is staked at its potential center once for all.

Christ as Creator was the Center of creation. The Spirit brooded over the void, giving form to it only from the Center. The Spirit in history is always centered in the One to come. The One who came is yet to come as history's fulfillment. Whatever highest revelation of Him, therefore, becomes available to man, becomes also for man the center of his conflict. Such a center is both the judgment of history and the hope of history. Man, at least on earth, never lives outside the circle of history. Instead, man lives in a concrete circle of history with a concrete center that is always the Christ. The Christ of Creation is the Christ of history's preparation until history be ready for the revelation of the Center itself. One layer after another is unfolded, until, by prophet and saint, history's center is made more intelligible. Concerning that center men must decide, at every stage, where to go in history. Thus concrete and timely are history's choices. History is the struggle of men for or against the center of their own circle. Sometimes a struggle may put layers of darkness over the center that was once bared and men may grope in a darker circle with less judgment and less hope. Sometimes those at the center, however, are allowed to uncover new layers of the center. Then the center and the new circle thus formed are both clarified, whereupon new struggles ensue within the new circle.

History is a matter of choice, *deep down,* for or against Christ the Center. He is the living force, whether through activities from beneath man or from above him. Man stands within the tension of Christ the Creator and Christ the Consummator within some circle of choice with regard to the concrete Christ of his own era. Pushed from below and pulled from above man must make decisions concerning the Christ. The purpose of history is the true purpose of Christ and of His Church, to create freedom and faithfulness in fellowship. The meaning of history is community. Man struggles for or against love, for man is made by and for Love. Man needs to be consummated by community. He needs to create fellowship.

To do so man needs time. Time must be real. It must mean the chance to make real choices from which man can grow. Time is the necessary means for such learning. Time is the prerequisite for freedom, just as freedom itself is presuppositional for history. History is the record of man's use of freedom and the challenge in the present for the creative use of that freedom. Time is the genetic means to community. Time is the accumulative means for self-realization. Time is the handmaid of God. Time is the condition of His grace. Time is "the heartbeat of God." Time is the chance to enter into the history of God and the heritage of free men. Time is the opportunity for learning to imitate God and to grow in love. History is a matter of choice, the choice for community. The necessary means for such choice and such community is time. God has plenty of time. The endless time of God may be the real reason that man rebels against God's seeming slackness while all the while His long-suffering is for man's salvation (II Pet. 3:9), through a freedom the extent of which we cannot now even begin to fathom.

---

[4] For a fuller discussion of time that underlies this chapter, see *The Christian Understanding of God*, chap. 4, "Time and Eternity."

Eternity is Christ-conquered time.[4] Our times are out of joint. They clash. They must clash in order for us to learn the true nature of time. Eternity is wherever God's purpose for community is realized. With Christ the Creator came time as the chance for choice. With Christ the God of history came time as the clash of choices and the learning of community. With Christ the Redeemer came time as the revelation of God's fullness. With Christ the Resurrection came time as that fullness actually obtained. With Christ the Consummator will come the time when God's will is done on earth as it is in heaven. Eternity has come into human time. Eternity keeps coming into human time through the living Christ. Eternity will fulfill and drastically alter human time when Christ the Consummator has subjected this cosmic age unto Himself and will Himself, as the Bible promises, be subjected to the Father in order that God be all in all.[5]

The goal of history is community: Community in Christ. The Center of history shows such community to be the most creatively intensive and the most numerically inclusive com-

[5] By time I mean an aspect of an event of life, of a person. Time is not substantive but adjectival. Eternity is God's time, an aspect of God's perfection. It is the infinite possibility in God and for God, of creative community and change. It is the succession of change that characterizes the Living God. Human time is an aspect of human life and human community, the genetic division of experience. It is the chance for choice and the opportunity for growing by the watching of the consequences of such choice. It is the means and media for community. God's eternity is, therefore, as Bishop Aulén holds, God's sovereignty over all times and conditions, but for me it is particularly the creative consummation of all created time. There is in my view nothing of the classical Greek view of eternity as the timelessness of God. I start, rather, with the Christian presupposition of the Living God, and work out time as adjectival to His life.

munity possible. The goal of history is, therefore, the Church. The Church is Christ-centered community. Whatever other kinds of community there may be, they all have their potential center in the Christ, but insofar as they are false or incomplete they are off center. At every stage of human history the Christ thus far revealed is the judging center of that history and the demanding pattern for that community. The central conflict of history is therefore the struggle for or against the Church of God. The Church, the universal and outgoing community, is in any age the circle nearest the center of human history. The Church is itself tested only by Christ the Center, the universal Agape. The true Church lives through the Center as a community for all other communities, even as the Christ is for all, but the Church itself is tested and enabled only by the Christ. Actual "churches," or their members, no matter how high their profession, may be far from the Center.

The only members of the true Church are those who know and live the Agape life. Those who do so, always feel unworthy of reward and unmindful of desert. They do not feel superior nor judge others. The final judgment of man is the testing by the God of Agape according to the standard of Agape. The Christ who is Agape, the Godman, is ever the judge of all men. His judgment is also ever for the sake of Agape that each and every person may find the final meaning of life, the eternal life which shares endlessly the full creative harmony of Agape, God with man and man with men.

Heavenly history is the Christian consummation of community. Heaven is eternal history. Heaven is Christ-conquered and Christ-filled time. It is God's resting with man on the Sabbath day. It is creation complete with consummation. It is history within the full purpose of God. Heaven is love complete with holiness. It is justice completed by love. It is love in perfectly concentric circles of humanity, with Christ at the center. Heaven is here and now, and then and there, within history and at its end. It is atonement made perfect by resurrection. It is time consummated by eternity. Heaven is history fulfilled.

Christ is thus the Consummator of history. Yet history, being big with time, never ends. It cannot end, because God is the ever-living, creative Love. His resources are exhaustless. History is consequently the eternally pregnant creation whereby time is ever reborn. History never began nor can it end. While God enjoys His sabbath at week's end, every sabbath comes to a close and God is eternally fresh on Monday morning. History keeps moving.

III. CHRIST, THE CONSUMMATOR OF CREATION AND HISTORY

Christ is not only the "crucified Creator" and the Lord of history, for he is also the Consummator of history. Here we gaze at dark depths of mystery. We see only a central Light that shines straight into the abyss. The deeper it penetrates, the thicker and more immense the darkness appears, but the darkness, to think with the Gospel according to John, can never throw it out. That central Light, rather, will keep shining and growing until the darkness is dispelled. Such victory is an end without an ending!

History never ends. There is no such thing as static history. There is no final consummation as the end of all time. Christ, rather, is the Consummator of our human history and of every history, in His time and way. God goes on loving and thereby creates ever new history. He is the God of Love who keeps creating. The Son is not begotten in time; time is begotten with Him. There is no time when the Father is not begetting the Son. The fact that the Son will in the end be subjected to the Father means that creative and final history is consummated as heavenly history: history in direct relation to and according to the full will of the Father. The nature of God is eternally to create in the exhaustless infinities. The nature of God is to love eternally. The nature of God is ever to beget His Son.

Nor does creation cease to change. History is constant change, for history is confluence and development of experience. This order of nature as such may disappear when its functions have been performed, but we await not only new heavens but a "new earth," new opportunities for creaturely history. The life of the redeemed community goes on. Continuing history is just such ongoing life. The communion of the saints in glory is heavenly history.

History, however, will be cleansed. It will be rid of its impurities and imperfections. It will be free of sin. The history of consummation is the experience of the perfected

Christian community. Christ the Consummator expunges from history all that falls below God's will for it. There will be relative conditions, to be sure, for the created remains created. There will be finitudes, for we never become God. But heavenly history will be free of its restlessness. The Sabbath will be a real experience. There remains a rest for the people of God! In this consummation we shall not be beset by such weariness of human life as we now know, where the other life seems, if not unreal, almost a thing to be dreaded. We shall not then be beset by the fever of life, where we can never really enjoy the Sabbath rest and the cool of the evening. We shall work and not weary; we shall rest and not fret. In this life we have foretastes of such attainment when in Christ we work and find work restful; when in Christ we rest and find our rest a work of grace; when in Christ we are burdened for the world and find our burden light. What such an experience can mean in its fullness, however, we cannot tell. We can only wait, and waiting bless God. No one can hope to spell out the conditions of consummation, but we can know the kind of conclusion to history, for we know God.

When we look ahead, the new that cannot be predicted in terms of what we now know must always seem paradoxical. No age can envisage what is beyond it, not only in time but in full reality. What has not been before is to us as though it were not. As we look back, we can see that the new has come, and we cannot imagine what life would be like if the new that we now know were not here. In such a case we should not be here ourselves! We are ourselves very new in the history of the cosmos, let alone of creation! Yet when we look forward we cannot imagine the new that is to be. We can only trust, and trusting accept what may come to us in this life and beyond this life. Looking ahead, we see that the new is beyond our comprehension by virtue of its being really new and therefore unpredictable in principle by what we now know. Yet when the fulfillingly new has come, we shall rub our eyes at our incredible ignorance and within that new existence render new service and new praise.

Reason is enlarged only by revelation, for reason depends on existence. Reason must have content. When the new has come, we shall be able to reason about it. Reason is not only form. Reason is also formed by fact. We shall know as we are known only when He who knows us takes us up into His fullness and completes in us the work of His Spirit. Faith can trust beyond seeing, but faith can find only by seeing. When the perfect is come that which is imperfect shall be done away. Only when the perfect has come, shall we see the full revelation. Then alone shall reason be satisfied.

Both reason and conscience, moreover, are restless in this life and beset by problems because revelation coming through Christ and the Holy Spirit awaits its consummation. To be sure, our response is part of reason and conscience. Response is *to* fact but *by* man. When our transformation into the new order beyond every present limitation has taken place, and when beyond death, physically and in the spirit, we have found the fuller revelation of God, our reason and conscience will both be satisfied by His presence and by His rule. Now, to think biblically, we see not the subjection of all things to Christ but we see Jesus! *Then* we shall see Jesus and all things subjected unto him. Agape will have won and will reign in matchless splendor and majesty. Then alone will reason be fully enlarged by revelation and conscience fulfilled by the completed and cleansed image of God.

Yet we know that we shall be even as Christ is. Therefore the unknown is known at its heart. We cannot foretell what eye has not seen nor ear heard but we can understand the fact that whatever be the presence and reign of God as Agape it can only be the occasion for our constant gratitude. Again, in the exultant words of Richard Baxter's hymn:

> Christ leads me through no darker rooms
> Then He went through before.

Those who do not sing of the future beyond the grave have known no heavenly present on this side of the grave. Those who await no life after death know no Christian consummation now. Those who know no consummation in the present have no full Gospel now. Those who do have the Gospel know *now* the joy and peace of believing; therefore they sing *now* the song of law and grace, of "Moses and the Lamb"; yet the full chorus can peal forth only when beyond death and beyond our kind of time, we shall all be even as Christ is.

Christ is the Conqueror of all history and histories. Christ is Love, and Love never fails. To say that Love fails is to insult God. To say that Love can fail is not to worship God as Agape, the final End as well as the only Source of life. But Love does fail of consummation in this life. Love fails immeasurably with us all. We die sinners, publicans and pharisees. Few die translated saints! In only a few has Love finished the radical remaking which seems humanly compatible with Agape. Therefore, since Love cannot fail but does fail in this life, our present life is the mere beginning. Life on earth is barely the start of the pilgrimage. Life on earth is the infantile attempt at walking. Life on earth is important, to be sure, even as infancy is important. But even as no infant is expected to pass the Graduate Record examinations, God's tests for us here and at the end of this life are the tests for primary pupils. Beyond earthly life lies the larger school where we are expected to mature according to new conditions.

It is certainly important both to God and to us that here on earth we pass our examinations as best we can. Life always is as serious as can be because God Himself is the examiner. What makes decision serious is not the length of our earthly days but the ever-inescapable God. He who thinks that not God but death settles our fate, believes more in human life than in God. We shall never have anything but a now, and we shall never be promoted except we pass our tests. Life is decision, and the consequences of wrong decisions are real. They are real to love, and they are real for the record. They are real also for the treatment that must follow. No one can escape the consequences of sin. Life is no one-way escalator!

But this life is no final examination at the end of life's full story. Salvation is being right with God and such rightness will take unimaginable time to achieve. God's grace is full beyond any history we can imagine. Yet even now we can become right in intention. We can learn now to feel the heartbeat of God and to entrust ourselves to His strong arm. Thus to know and to accept God is life's truest lesson and most meaningful decision.

The Parousia, the Presence of God in consummation, the "Second Coming," is an event in time. Whatever God does, He does in time. Time is the medium for God's action and man's. We know, however, that our kind of time will end. The end of our time will be its transformation into another kind of time. Time is the opportunity for being together, for knowing each other over a duration. Human time in particular is the chance for learning from our past experience how to live together in a better way.

Time as opportunity for community and fellowship over a duration will go on, but one day we shall have no need of time for learning from the past. Human time is school time, but eternity is not. We shall all be graduated. No people will hang on to school forever. In any case, we shall all come to the end of our moral education; God's work of disciplining us will be over. With our graduation human time will cease. Perhaps in some sense we shall be graduated at different stages; perhaps nevertheless we shall all appear at some common Commencement exercises. God seems to treat us both individually and together. To separate each person from history is wrong; to merge each person in common history is also false. There seem to be reasons both for individual treatment and for the epochal treatment of history. Freedom and faithfulness in fellowship require that both the personal and the social be given adequate emphasis. Yet what form future life, future judgment, and future graduation will take we cannot spell out. *God alone knows what He has in store for us.*

We do know, however, as surely as we know that God is God and God is Agape, that the full consummation will come. He cannot be defeated for Love cannot fail. He who doubts the very analytical implications of God doubts God. Not to believe in full consummation insults the character of God or sells the power of Christ short. Sin is too stubborn and freedom too real for easy victory. Nor will God force our freedom. Yet certainly Christ will not fail. We know that! God has endless resources and endless time. Such resources and time cannot save, of course; only God can. Nevertheless all time and all resources stem from God as their Source, and are in the service of the infinite Wisdom who created responsibly in love and who knows how to consummate His creation in love. Christ is by biblical definition the Love that never ends nor fails. Creation, revelation and redemption are fulfilled only by resurrection. Resurrection is not only over death but over all God's enemies. The final resurrection can mean nothing less than the victory of Christ over all his enemies; the final victory of universal Love is universal salvation.[6]

Christology is discouraging unless it dares pull out all the stops on the celestial organ and lets the music swell. Christology is deceit except it end in a hallelujah chorus. Too often we think, speak and write as though Christology were analytical geometry or experimental psychology. Christology is only for those who are Christ-conquered and Spirit-led. In the final analysis it is only for the adorers at the feet of the dying Christ and at the door of the open tomb. Christology is only for those who look into the heavens for the return of the same Christ who once ascended to the right hand of God: only those, that is, who in living faith believe that suffering Love is all-conquering. Love alone can write appropriate Christology; for Christology is not only the analysis of Love come to earth but the adoring acceptance of Him who came.

The wonder of Christology is stars in the eyes of the worshiper, for the Star of Heaven has led him to the humble manger. The Star of Heaven, though really there, is seen

---

[6] For a fuller biblical and theological treatment see my *The Christian Understanding of God*, chap. 9, "The Work of God in Last Things," and *Evil and the Christian Faith*, chap. 12, "Evil and Last Things."

only in the eyes of a child of God, the "starry-eyed" in Christ. That God becomes man is life's greatest and most wonderful mystery. The wonder of Christology is the mystery of the human acceptance of God; on the praying Jesus comes the heavenly Dove. The wonder of Christology is the marvel of temptations conquered by the presence of God. The wonder of Christology is the glory of human healing by the miracle of God's presence. The wonder of Christology is the presence of the face of God in the midst of human sin. The wonder of Christology is the heart of God, forgiving, empowering, and freeing man from his heaviest burden. The wonder of Christology is the reality of the transfiguration of ordinary life even while life's humble mission awaits below the mount of glory. The wonder of Christology is the cry of travail in a garden, the cry of agony on a cross, and the cry of victory as the angel descends to roll away the stone. The wonder of Christology is the waiting for the final victory by scorned Love and the transfigured glory of accepted Love where none shall stand outside it.

The final wonder, however, is beyond our present ken and feel. The glory of Christology is the fact that God as Son comes now to each one of us to forgive, to enable and to transform. The joy of Christology is that we, too, can know the presence and power of the eternal, only begotten Son of God. The radiance of Christology is that Love has lit up our dark sky to show us our malady and God's remedy for it.

The new Age of universal love is already here, awaiting only our acceptance. Christ stands now at our individual, church, community, racial, national and world doors, knocking for admittance. What wonder of reality that God still becomes enmanned. What better can any man ask of life? Nothing better; only more and more of His presence "until the perfect day."

INDEX

Acts, 38
Adam, 73
Agape, 10, 24 n., 28, 41, 50, 53 ff.,
 76, 93, 114 ff., 128, 129 n., 135
 n., 137, 143, 164 ff., 173, 175
 178, 186, 209, 213 ff., 239, 244
 ff.
anakephalaioosis, 95 ff.
anhypostasia, 95, 98 ff., 102 ff.
Anselm, 226
Apollinaris, 43 ff., 108, 184 n.
Aquinas, 77 n., 123
Arians, 39
Athanasius, 33, 44, 184 n., 202 n.,
 206
Athenagoras, 59 n., 209
Atonement, 12, 135 ff., 141 ff.
Augustine, 77 n., 110, 157, 186, 202
Aulén, 28, 40, 78, 185, 238 n.

Baillie, 77, 97, 190 n
Barclay, 20
Barth, 21, 29, 37, 42, 56, 77 n., 79
 n., 85 n., 86 n., 127, 196
Baxter, R., 93 ff., 195 n.
Berdyaev, 200 n., 205
Berkouwer, 91 n. ff., 125 n., 213 n.
Bible, 33 ff., 37, 49, 59 ff., 214
Bohlin, 225
Brightman, 20, 149
Brown, W. A., 25

Brunner, 60, 78, 107, 108 n., 135 n.,
 210 n.
Bultmann, 21, 51, 56, 56 n., 57, 144,
 183, 219
Butzer, 212

Cadbury, 21, 22
Calvary, 169 ff., 173, 185
Calvin, 22, 212
Camfield, F. W., 74
Carnell, E., 29 n.
Chalcedon, 42 ff., 124 n. ff.
Church, 28, 239 ff.
Cochrane, 74 n., 198 n.
Colossians, 38, 39, 172, 223 n.
Constantinople, 42 ff., 103, 116
II Corinthians, 90
Cranfield, C. E. B., 200 n.
creation, 141 ff., 225 ff.
Creator, 39, 223 ff.
creeds, 64 ff.
Cross, 60, 64, 81, 141, 163, 170, 181,
 230
crucifixion, 225
Cyril, 44, 95, 107, 116, 120 n., 178 n.

Denman, H., 154
Deutero-Isaiah, 59
Diekamp, F., 77
doceticism, 50
Duchesne, 100 n.

251

Earl Lectures, 11, 12
ecumenical councils, 41 ff.
Elias of Crete, 167
Elliot Lectures, 12
Emmet, Dorothy, 55 n., 85 n.
enhypostasia, 95, 106 ff., 114 ff.
Ephesians, 175
eros, 63, 137
Essenes, 160
Event-meaning, 24, 54, 58, 67
Everett, 149
evil, 229 ff.
existentialism, 27 ff., 69 ff.
experience, 24 ff.
Ezekiel, 156

Farmer, 129 n.
Fathers, 44, 65
Findlay, J. N., 71 n.
Forsyth, 25, 27, 51, 146

Galatians, 126
Gilkey, L., 63 n.
God (Christ as), 38
Godman, 45, 74 ff., 94, 107, 112, 114
    ff., 133 ff., 185, 197, 204, 219,
    239
Gregory Nazianzus, 96, 103, 108
Gregory of Nyssa, 118 n., 190
Grensted, 93, 129 n.
Grou, J. N., 172

Haire, J. L. M., 78
Hardy, 32, 46, 74, 76, 96, 135, 178
    n., 208 n.
Hebrews, 40, 84, 85, 89, 102 n., 111,
    177, 198 n.
Heidegger, 70
Hendry, 138 n., 139 n.
Hinduism, 150
history, 35 ff., 57 ff., 67, 213 ff., 225,
    232 ff.

Holy Spirit, 30, 33, 202 ff.
homoiousios, 42, 44
homoousios, 42, 44
Hoskyns, 94
hypostasis, 118

idealism, 27
Ignatius, 73
Incarnation, 9, 47, 50, 58, 75, 90, 98,
    99, 101 ff., 112 ff., 125, 125 n.,
    126, 128, 132, 134, 137 ff., 184
    ff., 193, 211, 214 ff., 225
Irenaeus, 74, 95 ff., 125, 177 n., 206

James, 111, 156
John (St.), 103, 105, 146, 208 n.
I John, 84, 198
John of Damascus, 208 n.
Jonah, 59
Jones, G. V., 39 n., 40, 84 n., 99 n.

Kantianism, 69
Kantonen, 224
Kierkegaard, 20, 56, 126 n., 192 n.,
    206 n.
kerygma, 40, 84 n.
Kingdom of God, 23, 112
Knox, John, 29

Laslett, 120
Leo, 189 n.
Leontius of Byzantium, 95
Leviticus, 59
logos, 39
Luke, 87
Lundensians, 28 ff.
Luther, 182, 212, 214 n.

Mark, 88, 127
Mascall, 210 n.
Matthews, W. R., 88 n.
Melancthon, 143
Messiah, 38

Index

$3.75

Christ
and the Christian

BY NELS F. S. FERRÉ

To help the reader understand Christ
in the many ways that men have conceived Him, and in so doing to become
more fully a Christian, is the intent
of this new and significant book. In it
a major theologian pleads for a real
Christ, not a theological construction;
at the same time Dr. Ferré, as a devout
believer, lays the basis for a logical and
systematic Christology.

"A revolution in Christology and in
religious thought," he writes, "will
take place when Christianity dares to
become radically Christian. Nothing
short of such a revolution will discover
and conserve the truth that both sets
men free and leaves them secure in
Christ."

Hence Dr. Ferré searches Biblical and
classical Christianity to show how it
reveals a universal relationship between
God and man, accepting the historic
uniqueness of Jesus as well as the fulfillment of God's presence in the
world today. When these are under-

(Continued on back flap)

No. 8005A